BARGAIN HUNT

BARGAIN HUNT

SPOTTER'S GUIDE TO ANTIQUES

KAREN FARRINGTON

BOOKS

1 3 5 7 9 10 8 6 4 2

BBC Books, an imprint of Ebury Publishing
20 Vauxhall Bridge Road,
London SW1V 2SA

BBC Books is part of the Penguin Random House group of companies
whose addresses can be found at global.penguinrandomhouse.com

This book is published to accompany the television series
entitled Bargain Hunt, broadcast on BBC One.

Executive Producer: Paul Tucker

Text by Karen Farrington
Illustrations by Judy Stevens

First published by BBC Books in 2022.
This edition published by BBC Books in 2022.

www.penguin.co.uk

A CIP catalogue record for this book is available from the British Library

ISBN 9781785947858

Typeset in 12/17 pt Baskerville by Jouve (UK), Milton Keynes
Printed and bound in Great Britain by Clays Ltd, Elcograf S.p.A.

The authorised representative in the EEA is Penguin Random House
Ireland, Morrison Chambers, 32 Nassau Street, Dublin D02 YH68

Penguin Random House is committed to a sustainable future
for our business, our readers and our planet. This book is made
from Forest Stewardship Council® certified paper.

CONTENTS

FOREWORD

Bargain Hunt has been a staple of British television for over twenty years. In fact, it's so quintessential, I'm unable to pinpoint the first time I sat down to watch two teams – bedecked in red and blue fleeces – buy three items to take to auction in a bid to make a profit. If I were to guess, it was probably sometime between 2005 and 2010; those were my university years and, as I've learned, our programme is beloved by students (who may or may not consider *Bargain Hunt* to be the perfect 45 minutes of procrastination).

When my uni days were done, I was able to secure a trainee position at a Glasgow auction house. I remember my first day as though it were yesterday: I was shown around the galleries, made to feel very welcome and asked to assist the head of the jewellery department with some photography for an upcoming sale. There was no pressure, no need to stress.

With equal clarity, I can recall my first day as a *Bargain Hunt* expert: I was shown around the antiques fair, made to feel very welcome and asked to compete against one of the programme's most respected experts, Paul Laidlaw (a towering, charming figure in a Panama hat) as part of a beloved daytime competition that would soon be watched by millions of people both at home and abroad. Running on pure adrenaline, I was (easily) convinced by the blue team – two farmers – that buying a modern-day plough was a sensible idea. I seriously doubted the wisdom of that particular purchase but, as it transpired, there really was no need to stress; it turned a fantastic profit and sealed our victory over Paul and his reds. What a debut?!

That I would be asked back by the producers for a second attempt felt improbable at the time. Had I been told *then* that I would be co-presenting the programme just two years later, I would have displayed utter disbelief. In fact, I don't think I did believe the programme's long-serving Executive Producer, Paul Tucker when he called in 2015 to break that news. 'Surely not?' seemed like the only appropriate response.

Broadcast on BBC One for the first time in the year 2000, *Bargain Hunt* (presented then by the inimitable David Dickinson) swiftly garnered a loyal following.

David's tenure – although nothing short of memorable – was relatively short-lived compared to the twelve years Tim Wonnacott spent at the helm between 2003 and 2015. His indelible mark? The iconic end-of-episode kick, of course.

It was with a great sense of responsibility that my co-presenters and I stepped in to fill those big shoes. 'Co-protectors' seems like a more fitting title; for many, *Bargain Hunt* is simply a daytime favourite, but for countless others it is a programme around which they shape their entire day. There are the retired viewers, who consider the programme an essential part of their lunchtime routine; the new parents, who pray that the phone won't ring as they bounce sleepy babies on their shoulders and watch us with the subtitles on; the carers, who plan their daily visits to elderly relatives around our start time of 12:15 pm; the aforementioned students, for whom *Bargain Hunt* continues to provide endless, quality meme content; the 'glory-hunters', who tune in just in time for the auction; and those who work from home, who spend their well-earned lunch break in the company of experts and presenters who feel (as we're often told) like good friends.

While our show's broad appeal is undeniable – and while the rules of the game are easy to explain in a sentence or two – trying to elucidate exactly what these different demographics enjoy so much is less straightforward. Perhaps the fact that making a profit on *Bargain Hunt* is genuinely challenging is what appeals the most – if you've ever cheered on a team that's made a £1.50 profit, you'll know exactly what I mean. Or perhaps it's the notion that *anyone* is welcome to apply to appear on the programme – fill in just one form and before you know it, you and your housemate could be the stars of the newest *Bargain Hunt* meme (and the proud possessors of some very fine fleeces).

Or maybe it's the very real drama that can unfold. You see, the 45 minutes shown on television represent several days of filming. First, there's the 'buy day', then there's the 'auctioneer chat' and, finally, the auction itself. A lot can happen in that time; there's been one marriage proposal, a handful of breakups and even a few births between the antiques fair and the auction . . . you just never know exactly how an episode is going to play out.

But, then again, you do: two teams will buy three items to take to auction in a bid to make a profit. Some will, some won't. There will be those who listen to their experts and those who ignore their advice entirely. Some will use their allocated buying hour wisely, others will finish with one second left on the clock. The odd person will feel compelled to buy a plough, but most will stick with porcelain and 'proper' antiques. As their items go under the hammer, a bold few will shout words of encouragement to the bidders in the saleroom. Most, however, will mutter a determined: '*Come on!*' as they watch their selections go by. Some teams will make a tidy profit and some will make a mighty loss . . . either way, they could still come out on top.

No matter what, lunchtime each day will start with the words: 'Hello and welcome to Bargain Hunt' and will end with a joyous kick.

Long may it continue.

Natasha Raskin Sharp

INTRODUCTION

As a brisk wind circles a vast conference hall, *Bargain Hunt* contestants Katie (Nicholas) and Aisha (Francis) glide between busy aisles in an antiques fair with £300 bulging in their joint purse.

The fair at Detling in Kent has 300 stalls mushrooming over 3,000 square metres. Each stall has tens or hundreds of items on display, with the pair looking for just three that have profit-making potential. And the clock is ticking.

Despite having cash in hand, shopping has never seemed so difficult as the choices arrayed before them are apparently limitless. There are rusty buckets, sets of bed linen and lengths of lace; coins, clothes, carpets and candle holders; flat irons and fire guards; desks and tables; trays, trunks and tea sets. To one side there are shelves of glass vases in every shade and hue, to the other the glare of polished silver is blinding. For the mechanically minded, serried ranks of clocks, watches, barometers and metronomes might appeal. If bling's your thing, there is row upon row of necklaces, earrings, beads, bracelets and brooches.

Ringing in their ears is the challenge set by presenter Charlie Ross. Today, this team must select something that's been shaped in a mould. Then there's the 'big buy' on their shopping list, to cost more than £75. All in just one hour, a limit strictly adhered to by the programme makers. This isn't going to be as easy as it looks every day on lunchtime television.

Happily, help is at hand in the shape of Thomas Forrester, an auctioneer and programme expert who has been a regular on *Bargain Hunt* since its inception in 2000. He has enough instinct, knowledge and abundant humour to take the pain out of the process. If they make any unwise choices, it will be left to him to redeem the total with a purchase made from any funds they had left.

An antique is an object from a bygone age, at least a hundred years old according to most definitions. Although this is an antiques fair, the Bargain Hunters aren't restricted to items that are Edwardian or older. They can root out any vintage, classic or retro objects and artefacts that take their fancy. Quirky will even fit the bill if the price is right. The aim is to make cash when each of their carefully selected pieces goes under the hammer at a future auction. What will today's hot choices be?

A first stop was made to examine a Chinoiserie vase, a European adaptation of Oriental design that's been in and out of favour in Britain since it was first conceived in the mid-eighteenth century. This wasn't an especially aged specimen, nor was it the only one in the show. Katie and Aisha moved on. But something at the next stall caught Thomas's eye. The reclining brass Buddha, with its glass eyes, had definitely been cast, and so fulfilled Charlie's challenge, and its price ticket immediately put it into the big buy bracket.

Thomas used his loupe, the experts' handheld magnifying glass, to scrutinise the sparkling red and green band encircling the Buddha's head. Some of the glass chips were missing, but he felt sure it came from Cambodia and dated from the nineteenth century. While the figure's top hand was artlessly formed, it was nonetheless charming and he felt at auction it might make as much as £150. Katie and Aisha paid £75 for the heavyweight item, securing two of their programme challenges in one item.

Sixteen minutes had passed and one purchase was bagged. But there was still plenty to do and three pairs of eyes were rapidly raking over packed tables and shelves until an old camera caught Katie's eye. She had, Thomas confirmed, picked up a fascinating piece of social history. Experiments in photography took place throughout the first half of the nineteenth century but only after 1888, when George Eastman's Kodak company produced portable cameras and flexible film to replace cumbersome plates, did most people have the opportunity to try their hand at it. Although this Box Brownie probably dated from the 1930s, the range was ubiquitous for more than sixty years. Its pivotal role was to popularise photography for the masses, yet the price tag was a humble £8. However, when Thomas revealed there was little wriggle room in terms of possible profit, Katie turned her back on it.

As Thomas peeled off to scour a different aisle, Katie spotted another piece of mechanical history, this time an early calculator. It was clunky, like a typewriter, but it still worked. Most vintage calculators functioned via a crank handle, but with ranks of operating buttons, this London-made model from the 1930s, with a £35 price tag, was a bit more advanced than that and had steampunk appeal. At thirty-three minutes, the sale was made and the team had just one item to find, with a princely £190 remaining in their pockets.

It took nearly fifteen minutes to find the last item but, when they saw it, it was love at first sight. The object of their infatuation was a diamond and sapphire ring, set in 18-carat gold. It was, Thomas confirmed, an excellent choice. Not only did it have evergreen appeal but second-hand rings like this one were a form of recycling, so conformed to the green agenda.

'The stones have already been mined, the gold has already been dug out of the ground,' he said. 'Buying a ring like this one is helping to save the planet's resources.'

Art Deco in design, it dated from the 1940s. It was perfect in every respect – except for the fact that it cost more than they had left in their fund. Now the team, aware that time was ticking away, united to charm the stallholder into a price reduction that both sides could live with. Her first position of £190 was no good as it left Thomas with nothing with which to purchase his bonus buy item. There was more haggling to be done, until finally £189 was agreed, with a comfortable forty-seven minutes on the clock, leaving Thomas with £1 in his pocket for a bonus buy.

Just as the deal was struck, the rival blue team being led by Chuko Ojiri bundled past at speed. They were running out of time, with several purchases yet to be made, and had to make some decisions, fast. For Katie and Aisha, a well-earned cup of tea awaited them while Thomas went off and shopped for his bonus buy.

Undefeated by the pin money at his disposal, he returned with a ceramic bottle label on a chain specially made for sherry drinkers, confident he would at least double his money.

After the shopping is over, the next step is to take the haul to an auction. History has changed auction rooms irrevocably, with most starting life years ago selling rundown properties and farming stock. Today, a colossal range goes under the gavel – sometimes great works of art, although there are many more everyday items at pocket money prices.

Auctioneers, hammers and the lofty rostrum can inspire fear among first timers. This book will help to demystify the process, much as the programme does for the contestants. Usually, it's the first time *Bargain Hunt* teams have attended a professional auction – and they've got skin in the game. Did they buy wisely, or was their judgement skewed?

Their financial fate lies in the hands of the buyers at the auction. At the end of it, they will go home with their profits in their pockets – if they have any. If each of the three items they've chosen sells for more than they paid, they are awarded a 'golden gavel', a lapel pin that signifies their luck and antiques acumen. But alas, losses occur with more frequency than golden gavels. If the team loses money, well, it's written off as the titles roll at the end of the programme.

These days, it's not just people in the saleroom on the day that will determine their progress, but those standing by on the phone or on the internet. Sometimes bids are left with auctioneers from those who've viewed the day's lots beforehand but can't make the sale. Although the reach of the auction is extended, new platforms like the internet don't necessarily increase values, although they certainly widen the purchasing pool. Some items have regional appeal that enhances their value. Likewise, some auction rooms are simply less productive than others. It all goes into the mix to make for some nail-biting moments for teams who are left urging sellers on from the sidelines; whooping as the bids pour in or groaning as an ominous saleroom silence descends.

Bargain Hunt has changed since it first appeared on our screens in 2000 with presenter David Dickinson. It's now bookended by a different theme tune and titles and even the rules of the game have been refined since the days when viewers were typically silver-haired retirees.

Today, the programme has pace and adrenalin, and the contestants are as likely to be young fans who as children watched *Bargain Hunt* at the knees of their grandparents.

But some features about this Great British television institution remain the same. The first BH purchase ever made was a 1950s 'Everhot' Art Deco tea set for £34 and it's an item just as likely to attract interest today. Delving into the country's social history through a selection of spellbinding objects is just as captivating as it ever was. And a score that runs into minus three digits, may still be just enough to win.

Catchphrases from the Show

'Buy low, sell high.'

'Make a memory.'

'Now, those have to be cheap as chips.'

'A bobby dazzler.'

'Double bubble.'

'Let's go Bargain Hunting!'

'Join us for some more Bargain Hunting Yes? Yes!' (Kick)

'What's your favourite item?'

'What will make the biggest profit?'

'Not a word to the blues/reds . . .'

1

CERAMICS

Stacked on the shelves of a Devon antiques emporium were plates, cups and saucers that caught the eye of one contestant for their aching familiarity.

This was a part-set of Homemaker, a black-and-white design sold in quantity by Woolworths from the 1950s for two decades. The giant retail chain's branches once held ranks of plates and bowls, flan dishes and soup tureens, coffee pots and cruets, all distinguished by a creamy background decorated with inky cartoon drawings of household items. The cups alone were entirely black, reflecting the limitations in the printing processes of the era. It was monochrome crockery like this *Bargain Hunt* challenger saw at every mealtime as a child.

The distinctive design – branded 'iconic' by *Bargain Hunt* expert Stephanie Connell – was created by art student Enid Seeney, who lived and worked in the Potteries. A Woolworth's stock buyer discovered it on a trip to

Staffordshire and agreed to give the avant-garde pattern a trial run. Made from economical earthenware by Ridgway Potteries, it offered householders the opportunity to quickly and cheaply replace broken items. There were several different teapot designs, selling for between ten shillings and fifteen shillings (that's fifty pence and seventy-five pence today). Once mundane and now highly collectible, a teapot might command £200 at a sale today.

In this moment of nostalgia for the *Bargain Hunt* buyer, she parted with £35 for the incomplete tea set and it sold at the subsequent auction for £50, yielding a £15 profit, a testament to the enduring power of good design.

Since the dawn of time, mankind has fashioned clay cups and plates from natural elements. And almost since then, form as well as function has been a consideration. Ceramics is a catch-all phrase to describe items that are shaped, decorated, glazed and fired. Porcelain is part of the ceramics family, developed in China where a blend of white kaolin clay mixed with crushed stone could be fired at high temperatures to produce a product that was smooth and lustrous.

Using first the Silk Road through Asia and then fleets of junks, China was the world's foremost trading nation for many centuries, with porcelain among its major exports.

Chinese porcelain was highly sought after by Europeans, particularly the signature blue-and-white variety. At the time, the domestic choice was technically limited and far less elegant. The Delftware tin-glazed option was only available in Britain from the sixteenth century, after the process of mixing lead and tin into a glaze to form a white background was imported from the Middle East.

With Chinese merchants demanding payment in either silver or gold, Oriental pots were only purchased by the very rich. France's Louis XIV had all the silver at Versailles melted down to finance the import of porcelain, while Augustus the Strong, the Elector of Saxony, was so spellbound by it that he described himself as having 'porcelain fever'.

For centuries, no one in Europe recognised the vital role that kaolin clay played in making the Chinese hard-paste porcelain that inspired such a frenzy. Finally, it was in August the Strong's royal factory at Meissen, near Dresden, that a series of experiments led to the firing of Europe's first comparable white porcelain, in 1708.

Of course, the recipe didn't stay a secret and soon the French and British were producing a substitute of their own.

A century after the breakthrough at Meissen, British manufacturers took the concept in a different direction with bone china. Although it was translucent, it was stronger than hard-paste porcelain, despite a lower firing temperature.

Still, the lure of Chinese pottery didn't abate. The last half of the nineteenth century saw British fashionable society in the grip of 'Chinamania', a desire to own Chinese porcelain, despite the abundant alternatives available at home, something for which they were widely mocked in the press at the time.

There are plenty of Chinese-style ceramics available at antiques fairs today, which may be originals, copies or even outright fakes. The experienced eye of *Bargain Hunt* expert Ben Cooper is an asset for any team who might be bewitched by Chinoiserie.

When he isn't leading *Bargain Hunt* teams into battle, Ben sometimes finds himself working as an authenticator of Chinese ceramics at major antiques fairs.

'Generally, we expect to see British ceramics through history bear marks, as a way to identify the skill of the makers. With Chinese porcelain that isn't the case. Imperial porcelain might have blue rings on the bottom, or auspicious characters.'

Presented with a piece, experts like Ben will pick it up to scrutinise the shape, the decoration, the porcelain body and the colours, to determine whether it is genuine.

'With anyone who has a specialism, it becomes second nature,' he explains.

Chinese ceramics reached something of a high-water mark in the reign of Emperor Kangxi (1662–1722) and, in the nineteenth century, identical work was produced because he was so revered. So, to distinguish a replica from the real thing is no mean feat.

'The Chinese have been copying their historic porcelains for years,' says Bargain Hunt's Jonathan Pratt. 'Some suggest it is flattery, not forgery. However, there is a massive industry in China making copies of older pieces. They make their way to auction and fool many.'

But a number of original and rare Chinese pieces do turn up in sheds and lofts, so might you have a rare piece of Chinese artwork tucked away at home? The short answer is, yes.

'The British had a strong presence in China during the nineteenth century when there were two "Opium Wars" followed by a Chinese rebellion against foreign powers,' Jonathan, better known as JP, explains.

During these times, the soldiers involved collected small items and brought them home. Larger pieces of porcelain from looted palaces were also exported back. When these crop up at auctions today they cause a ripple of excitement that extends across the globe, with Chinese buyers keen to repatriate items.

Tales from the Auction House

Two plates retrieved from a suitcase under a bed in 2021 were sold by Caroline Hawley for £146,000. Marks on the plates led her to believe they were linked to a Qing dynasty emperor who ruled between 1722 and 1735. The five-clawed dragon image indicates the plates would have been made for the Imperial household. A buyer from the UK put in the winning bid.

Given its compelling history, it's hard not to view Chinese porcelain without unfettered admiration. An early love for antiques was cemented for *Bargain Hunt* expert Gary Pe when, as a young man, he bought a terracotta urn with its handles held in the teeth of sculpted beasts. Unmistakably Chinese, it had been unearthed in the Philippines, where he was brought up. There had been a busy trade route between the Philippines and China for centuries and, to prove it, here was a piece of Late Song or Early Ming pottery found on one of the islands. Admittedly, its glaze was partially gone but it was something that had likely been in existence since at least the fifteenth century, many decades before Europeans could produce porcelain for themselves. It was the first object he paid money for and he has kept it for more than forty years and across three continents.

In parallel to the fascination for Chinese artefacts came Japonism. Despite its rich cultural and economic life, Japan effectively existed in isolation until the arrival of an American fleet in 1853, which compelled the country's reluctant inhabitants to trade more briskly with the West. Afterwards, pottery makers catered both for export and internal markets, with imagery from Shinto, the dominant faith, appearing on numerous articles made for domestic buyers.

Perhaps more significantly still, the West discovered kintsugi, or golden joinery, an unusual feature of Japanese artefacts in which repairs to major pieces shine out, when in the West they are masked. Broken pieces were traditionally glued, and the joins richly painted with gold, silver or platinum powders before being lacquered. The bold lines that resulted spoke of the artefact's journey, and celebrated an inherent joy of imperfection. It left people in the West, bound to the idea of flawlessness, scratching their heads.

Oriental porcelain aside, Britain's home-produced merchandise also has a sterling band of supporters, with Worcester being the most widely collected eighteenth-century ceramic. The key period is the output of the Worcester factory in the first thirty-two years of its existence. It's known as the First Period, or the Dr Wall period, for the name of one of the company's original partners. (Indeed, it didn't officially become known as the Royal Worcester Porcelain Company until 1862.)

Initially, it was strongly associated with tableware and took its inspiration from Chinese and Japanese porcelain. But decorative innovations came in thick and fast, with floral, rococo and moulded decorations coming to the fore. Today, people might collect by patterns, type of decoration or date. When a rarely seen example is unveiled it brings enthusiasts to auction, explains JP.

'As a child, I collected Panini football stickers and there were always some missing that everybody wanted,' says JP. 'Early pieces of Worcester are like that, particularly those in rare shapes. When they turn up they make big money – but they don't turn up very often.'

Philip Serrell began his passion for Royal Worcester when he visited a museum as a child.

'When people look around museums at porcelain like this, they have to appreciate that, back in the middle of the eighteenth century when the first Royal Worcester pieces were made, it might have taken two days to reach London by coach, there was a sewer running down the main street and life expectancy was probably about forty years of age. Yet the men, women and children who worked in the ceramics factories were producing beautiful things. How did they do that?'

Royal Worcester and Royal Derby are the country's oldest porcelain makers. As people lose faith in currency, they are investing in antiques like Royal Worcester, explains Philip, and they get pleasure from the items they buy. He recalls a saying used by his first boss to help govern any investment: 'Let your eyes be your guide and your pocket be your judge.' 'It means: don't buy because everyone else is buying. Buy it because you like it, and because you can afford it,' he explains.

And, he says, it's still possible to purchase something made in the eighteenth century, perhaps in a characteristic blue-and-white pattern, for about £50. These days 'old' doesn't always equate to 'most valuable'. Today, the big money goes to the porcelain hand-painted in the early twentieth century by factory workers who have become acknowledged artists.

Harry Davis is a particular favourite for Philip, who insists: 'You can't find a better twentieth-century painter in my book.'

Best Buy

In 2006, Philip Serrell went to the top of the *Bargain Hunt* bonus buy charts after he seized on a Royal Worcester mini-masterpiece. The vase, with a painted scene of sheep on its side signed by Harry Davis, could fit into the palm of his hand. Davis had begun work as an apprentice for Royal Worcester in 1898, aged just thirteen. Two years later, the company permitted its artists to add a moniker to their paintings, so much of Harry's work, from the turn of the century until his retirement in 1969, aged eighty-three, can now be distinguished. When Philip realised the vase was in pristine condition, he knew he was on to a winner.

Bought £170 Sold £780 Profit £610

Best Buy

The silver framework of the trinket box was battered, but expert Michael Hogben revealed it wasn't the metalwork that counted in this instance, but the painted enamel plaque that sat in its lid. Hallmarks revealed that the box was made in Birmingham in 1928, while initials showed it was artist George Johnson, working for the historic Royal Worcester Porcelain Company, who was responsible for the delicate pair of flamingos in the picture. Despite wear and tear on the silver, presenter David Dickinson knew the find was 'a cracker', and a packed auction house agreed with him, propelling this piece to the top of the lots in Bargain Hunt history.

Bought £140 Sold £800 Profit £660

With a personal collection of antiques and curios that includes not only Royal Worcester but also a wooden leg made for a sheep, Philip insists he is not an expert but a generalist, although his knowledge has been gathered through forty-five years of auctioneering. He believes that there is still so much to find out about a world of antiques that, for him, brings social history to life. And he's not the only proud generalist on the show.

'Pottery is about designs, shapes, colours and makers,' says pragmatic Gary Pe. 'No one is the ultimate expert. Someone else will always know more.'

As Worcester products were making their mark, a new era for a different market was ushered in when Spode derived the technique for transfer printed pottery in the 1780s. Ceramic artists found themselves redundant after a design was engraved onto a copper plate, which was then transferred to plain earthenware with the use of a cobalt compound. The item was finally glazed and fired for a second time. Two printers were said to be able to do the work of a hundred painters. Moreover, the reduction in costs associated with underglaze transfer printing enabled more people to buy decorated dishes than ever before. Today, it is collected in themes; by design, shape, age or colour, with blue eventually being joined by green, brown, manganese, grey and black products. Such items don't summon up visions of a Regency society banquet, more a farm table feast. It remains popular in America, with the early export of dishes and bowls featuring patriotic scenes.

The choice for ceramics enthusiasts is as wide as the horizon and encompasses all kinds of tastes. Today, the value of china is dependent on its condition. Against expectation, bone china is surprisingly resilient, says Colin Young, with striking translucency. But the best test is to give it a tap. An item with a hairline fracture – one that might have been there since it was first fired – will return a dull thud. Bone china that has kept its integrity will have a distinctive ring. English-made china artefacts will likely bear a gilt decoration so should be kept out of the microwave, he advises, or sparks will fly.

Modern Britain developed its own styles and there are numerous notable examples. Perhaps the country's foremost pottery artist was Clarice Cliff. She was born in a terraced house in the Midlands at the dawn of the twentieth century and began work in the Potteries from the age of thirteen. After mastering gilding, she started freehand painting, while studying at an art college at night.

Before long, she pitched up at Newport Potteries, and started designing her own range. Against convention, she became known for bold colours and startling design, producing what presenter Eric Knowles calls 'sunshine pottery'. During a glittering career, she established 400 original shapes and 500 hand-painted patterns.

As Roo Irvine puts it: 'She burst onto the scene with bold, wild abstract colours. Growing up with a very humble background, her sheer determination, wonderful sense of colour and design, alongside an understanding of what the "It-Generation" at the time were looking for, helped secure her name in pottery history. There were as many fans as there were critics, but she broke the mould.'

In 1927 Cliff launched the Bizarre range. It was dubbed 'cheerful china' by the press and was less pricey than competitors. The team of decorators that covered angular teapots, pyramid sugar shakes and stepped vases with vivid oranges and startling yellows were called the Bizarre Girls.

Some Clarice Cliff pottery was produced in such great amounts it can be bought today for a relatively small amount. But examples from rarely found ranges are likely to attract much more money, as do trial pieces.

For a decade, Wedgwood brought out a range of Clarice Cliff reproductions, clearly marked as such. But, says Roo, fakes do exist and are made to such a high standard that they are very plausible. She has tips for verification that you can carry out at home:

1. First of all, check the shape against reference books, as crudely painted patterns can be added to any old pot or vase! The pattern should coincide with the right vessel!

2. Secondly, look at the colours – the very thing Clarice Cliff is celebrated for. They need to sing brightly, and her much loved Tango Orange was banned some time ago due to the high lead content in the paint so that colour would be very difficult to fake. Look at the quality of the painting – her decorators were highly skilled and it shows.

3. If you think you have found a rare pattern, be wary if it is priced under £100 – it is either completely undiscovered by the dealer, or not the real deal!

Eric adds another word of warning, that is, to be wary of sympathetic restoration. If you are buying, make sure the invoice stipulates it is in perfect condition in order to conserve value.

Clarice Cliff was not the only remarkable designer working in the Staffordshire potteries at the time. Born in the same neighbourhood, Susie Cooper also found fame for her significant contribution to the region's cultural development, working with earthenware as well as bone china.

Poole Pottery is another popular choice. After launching in 1873, Poole Pottery mostly produced architectural decorations. But in the twentieth century it became famous for floral, then abstract, designs.

Many early pieces can command high prices in the saleroom. Look out for early works marked by the names of Cyril Carter, Robert Adams and Truda Carter. Indeed, some pots designed and initialled by Truda Carter have been known to make four figure sums.

However, buying British is no guarantee of a profit. A team that fell in love with the peacock colours of a Minton Hollins vase, of an uncertain vintage, willingly paid £35. But when it went to auction, it sold for just £20, producing a £15 loss. Minton remains a solid brand. However, profits and losses are governed by who turns up in the auction room on the day.

Moorcroft is another distinctive British brand that has a band of devoted fans. Initially, William Moorcroft began his career working for Staffordshire pottery James Macintyre & Co, where he used bold blues, reds and golds to distinguish his designs. After that, he used a process called tube lining, a drawn-out process but one that gave Moorcroft pottery a distinctive charm. Eric Knowles explains the steps involved.

'He put liquid clay, the consistency of thick cream, through a rubber bag, which was trailed onto the pot following stencilled lines. Once that had dried, it was then fired. After being painted it was fired again. Then the glaze was applied and it was subjected to a final firing.'

Moorcroft began a business of his own, forging successful links with the London department store Liberty & Co. Since then, his company has been through several incarnations, producing pottery that remains popular and collectible.

Measham ware is another distinctive British marque, named for the village where it was sold, which stands on the Ashby Canal. These rustic earthenware items, also known as bargeware, were mostly made in Church Gresley, Derbyshire, between 1870 and the outbreak of the First World War. They are distinctive for their thin glaze and bleeding colours. Mostly remembered for teapots, Measham ware also includes tobacco jars, jugs, sugar bowls and chamber pots. They often bear greetings and were usually brought as gifts rather than for use on a barge.

Imitations can be distinguished from the real thing as the glaze is thinner and better applied, the messages are painted on rather than imprinted and the bottom of reproductions is a different colour to the original.

Troika pottery was made in Cornwall from the 1960s and remains distinctive as textured earthenware in muted colours. Items were made in moulds and bore handwritten marks on the bottom. The Troika enterprise closed in 1983. One *Bargain Hunt* pair stumbled upon a Troika vase that they snapped up for £75. At auction it sold for £85, meaning a £10 profit.

More modern still is the Leonardo Collection, a brand of houseware and collectible figures launched in 1971.

Certainly, beauty is in the eye of the beholder and, given the vast range available, ceramics are no different.

Which brings the topic around to Toby jugs – bold, leering and ubiquitous. Today, the era of the toby jug is behind us but still, they have a place in the story.

According to Roo, although the idea has ancient roots, they grew out of the Georgians' love of drink. This was, after all, the same era that satire through caricatures came of age, and the idea of skewering stereotypes was a popular one.

There's an important descriptive distinction to be drawn here at the start: a toby jug has a large face and a squashed body, while a character jug depicts just the head and shoulders.

'During the 1760s, Staffordshire potters developed the toby jug. No single potter is credited as they were vastly made due to their popularity and usage in pubs and taverns. They were an early form of materialistic consumerism and mass production at a time when technology was booming,' Roo explains.

Manufacturing bases spread across the nation and the Kircaldy-based Methvens Pottery even made toby jugs in tartan. But, more typically, the toby jug epitomised the roguish Georgian drunkard.

'The cleverly crafted face depicted signs of excessive living – pockmarks, missing teeth and a ruddy complexion. Dressed in eighteenth-century clothes, wearing a tricorn hat and accessorised with a mug of beer and a pipe, the drunkard's tricorn hat featured a spout, making it perfect for pouring, hence they were jugs rather than mugs.'

Roo urges today's toby jug owners to look upon them with pride and, while they are indisputably unfashionable, there might still be a small amount of value attached to them.

'Early jugs show paintbrush marks. Hollow feet on the base are often pre-1840. Commemorative jugs of Royal and Political figures are also very collectible.'

Royal Doulton became known for making character jugs and figures in the twentieth century. The company's head of design was Charles Noke and from 1934 he oversaw the launch of a range of character jugs, in three sizes. Subjects ranged from Winston Churchill to Garfield the Cat and, if in doubt, the name usually appears on the bottom. In general terms, there is a glut on the market, which reduces their value considerably, although rarities needed to complete collections can spark a bidding war at auction.

Some subtle variations make one character jug stand out from the crowd. There have been numerous versions of an aged woman modelled with a single tooth protruding between her lips. One *Bargain Hunt* team seized on just such a 'granny' mug, with a £5 price tag. At auction it sold for £40. However, some versions have her without a tooth showing at all, and these are rarer and thus even more valuable. Unusual colour combinations might also mark out a character jug from the rest.

It's impossible to describe all the British china and ceramics that buyers stumble across in today's antiques market. If its maker hasn't been mentioned, that's not to say that the arty vase that has stood on your mantelpiece for years isn't an undiscovered gem in the world of ceramics. If you think it may be, get it valued. But if you like it, you might just prefer to leave it where it stands.

Analyse That: Age and Period

When it comes to valuation, *Bargain Hunt* expert John Cameron has derived a way to turn an art into a science, through careful analysis. Here he shares the step-by-step formula he provides for newcomers to the antiques arena, to guide them when it comes to buying and selling.

Determining the age and period of an object is often the first piece of the jigsaw to establish. It is usually expressed by the century in which it may have been made or the reigning monarch of the time. Using the words 'seventeenth century' is how we would describe an item made during the 1600s and 'eighteenth century' means an item made during the 1700s. With experience one can be more precise, using 'late eighteenth century' or 'first quarter of the nineteenth century' and so on. Having a basic knowledge of the reigns of British monarchs is also a must for the would-be valuer, for when a prefix of the century isn't used, the name of a monarch is normally used instead. Likewise, the prefixes 'late Victorian' or 'Early Georgian' are also applied. Below are the dates and periods of British monarchs from Elizabeth I in the sixteenth century to George V in the early twentieth century.

Monarch	Dates	Period	Style
Elizabeth I	1558–1603	Elizabethan	Gothic
James I	1603–1625	Jacobean	Gothic
Charles I	1625–1649	Carolean	Baroque (1620–1700)
Commonwealth	1649–1660	Cromwellian	
Charles II	1660–1685	Restoration	
James II	1685–1688	Restoration	
William & Mary	1688–1694	William & Mary	
William III	1694–1702	William III	Baroque/ Rococo
Anne	1702–1714	Queen Anne	Rococo
George I	1714–1727	Early Georgian	
George II	1727–1760	Mid Georgian	
George III	1760–1811	Late Georgian	Rococo/Neo Classical
George III	1811–1820	Regency	Empire/ Regency
George IV	1820–1830	Regency	Regency
William IV	1830–1837	William IV	Eclectic
Victoria	1837–1901	Victorian	Various Revivals/ Arts & Crafts

Monarch	Dates	Period	Style
Edward Vll	1901–1910	Edwardian	Sheraton Revival/Art Nouveau
George V	1910–1936		Arts & Crafts/ Art Deco

Although age is the first piece of information that would appear in the description of an item, in, say, an auction catalogue or valuer's inventory, this is only really confirmed once we have considered most of the other criteria, such as the 'style', but especially the materials and construction techniques employed. Of equal importance is an understanding of the religious and political backdrops of each period, for this will also prove invaluable in putting the puzzle together.

2

JEWELLERY

*A*s a blinding light flashes from the surface of an engagement ring, it's apparent a diamond is the centrepiece of this antique love token. Or is it?

The world's most enduring and expensive jewel, the diamond has long been associated with special occasions. However, it is also often imitated by white sapphires, cubic zirconia, laboratory-grown synthetic alternatives – and glass.

Happily, the experts on *Bargain Hunt* won't be fooled. Expert valuer Kate Bliss, one of several qualified gemologists in the team, explains just what she's looking for when she gets out her loupe:

1. We can judge a diamond by the four Cs – Carat, Colour, Clarity and Cut. The first is carat, or weight, the feel of it on the palm of the hand.

2. Then there's colour. Many stones are tinged yellow by the nitrogen content of the mine they were taken from. The whiter the colour, the more highly prized the stone.

3. Next comes clarity. As the diamond is being formed under the earth's crust, it may well end up locking in some imperfections. The best diamonds are flawless.

4. Finally, there's the cut of the diamond, which as the hardest stone known to us, will have crisp lines. Softer stones will after time have rounded facet edges. A diamond will stay knife-edge sharp forever.

Each stone is judged in those four categories, although only the best achieves a high score in each. Beyond that, there are more nuanced clues to look for as well. For example, imperfections, known as inclusions, might detract from a diamond's value but also help to distinguish diamonds from other stones. There are further signs, like the brilliance of the light as it plays on the surface of a diamond. Moissanite, one of the man-made lookalikes, gives more of a disco ball effect, while glass reflects much as a windowpane might.

If you are keen to plunder jewellery stalls at your local antiques fair, it's well worth investing in a loupe like Kate's, which, for a cost of about £20, will offer at least ten times magnification.

Today, diamonds are cut by machine. In Georgian times, before the age of mechanisation, scrutinised diamonds might have evidence of the natural outer skin that once surrounded them, another clue as to a gemstone's journey. Kate has years of experience, but she's still fascinated by the look and feel of diamonds. For her, a photograph – while it might work in the valuation of a vase, for example – simply won't do when it comes to diamond jewellery. And her advice is to always get gemstones checked by an expert, so you know just what's in your jewellery box.

One of her clients popped in on the way to a charity shop, ready to donate an array of inherited items but wisely thought to ask Kate to look at the haul before giving it away. And there, beneath a pile of costume jewellery, was a Victorian diamond star brooch, ultimately auctioned for £3,500.

Conversely, the 'diamond' necklace inherited from a great aunt who always insisted it was laden with precious stones might amount to little more than a showy piece, if someone has previously cashed in on the gems. And when times were hard – during the Great Depression of the twenties, for example – some people did replace valuable stones in the family jewellery with paste and traded in the gems. If stealthily made replacements were a decent imitation, no one would notice the switch. There's no point paying insurance on an inherited diamond tiara if it is in fact virtually worthless, so get any inherited trinkets checked.

Synthetic diamonds have a similar chemical composition to mined ones but can be grown in laboratories rather than dug out of the ground. They are not fakes but nor are they the same as the real thing, explains Kate. Moissanite has some mystical romance about it, being first discovered inside a meteorite, but this 'space diamond' is now grown inside. It is an ethical alternative to diamonds but worth a fraction of their value. Lab-grown diamonds like this may well be marked 'LG' to denote their provenance.

With her dad an auctioneer, Kate used to return from school to rummage in boxes of newly acquired antiques destined for the saleroom. After getting an English literature degree at university, she returned to the world of antiques and set about acquiring a range of professional qualifications to enhance her working knowledge. She became one of the country's first female auctioneers and has worked on *Bargain Hunt* since the programme began.

Another generation of female auctioneers is now following in her footsteps, among them Izzie Balmer, who chose the career after two weeks' work experience spent at an auction house.

When it comes to jewellery, Izzie advises people to buy the best they can afford. 'Buy something you like and don't think of it as an investment. Antiques' values can go up and down, so wear it, cherish it, love it.'

And just as diamonds can be mimicked, so can pearls – and it's not always easy to distinguish the real thing.

Pearls are made inside small animals, rather than in the ground. Natural pearls occur spontaneously when a bit of grit or a parasite finds its way into the shell of one of twenty pearl-producing molluscs. To counter the disturbing effect of the irritant, the creature covers it with nacre, made from calcium carbonate, the same ingredients that coat the smooth and shiny insides of their protective shells. The process takes years and natural pearls like these are rare and valuable.

In 1893, Kokichi Mikimoto from Japan discovered he could kick-start the creation of pearls by inserting an artificial irritant into a farmed mollusc. The result is a cultured pearl and it's hard even for experts like Izzie to distinguish one from the natural variety.

'Sometimes you can see the inserted bead around which a cultured pearl has formed, but not always. Of course, that bead is absent in a natural pearl. You would have to get a pearl X-rayed to be sure.'

Initially, people were perplexed by cultured pearls and the way they were created, so much so that Mikimoto found himself in a French court, defending the process. And after he triumphed in the legal fight, his jewellery – a fusion of Japanese and European styles and marked with an 'M' inside the outline of an oyster shell – became popular everywhere.

There's even an acknowledged divide between pearls cultured in fresh or salt water. Those grown on riverbeds may be more egg-shaped than their ocean-sourced equivalents.

Beyond natural and cultured pearls, there are simulated ones, which tend to have a different lustre than the real thing. 'Good simulated pearls may have a fish bone covering to make them look more realistic,' says Izzie. 'But it doesn't increase their value.'

Prone to damage by perfume and hairspray, it's advisable to wait fifteen minutes after using the sprays before putting on your pearls, Izzie warns. And pearls don't generally store that well.

'Pearls need to be worn,' says Izzie. 'Pop them on during the day, beneath a jumper, so they can soak up the oils on your skin. You won't see a difference straight away but over time each will look like a real pearl again, rather than something that's dull or flat.'

Tales from the Auction House

Peter Carl Fabergé – whose name is synonymous with exquisite gems and precious metals – was not only known for exotic and bejewelled regal Easter eggs but also for other contributions to the decorative arts. Charles Hanson experienced a moment that every auctioneer dreams of when he opened a shoebox and folded back the tea towels inside to reveal two Fabergé flowers. The first was a Morning Glory Convolvulus, with tiny diamonds set into its enamel petals, on a stem protruding from a marble base. A matching model is in the Royal Collection. Then there was a barberry bush, produced by Henrik Wigström, who was a craftsman in the Fabergé stable. The treasures had once been the property of Lady Duff, a prominent member of Britain's elevated society, and had descended through her family to a distant relative. Charles found archive references to each piece to prove their provenance. When it came to auction, the Convolvulus sold for £180,000 and the barberry bush for £160,000.

In Victorian times, pearls sometimes featured in mourning jewellery, which became high fashion, not least because it was worn by Queen Victoria after the death of husband Albert in 1861. However, the most commonly found mourning jewellery is black, engraved with significant dates or may feature a lock of hair. Somewhat chillingly, it's called *memento mori*, meaning: 'Remember, we are all going to die'.

Yet for *Bargain Hunt's* Roo Irvine, it's a fascinating area of history. 'A lot of people find it weird and macabre but I think it's romantic,' she says. 'It is born out of love and passion. This was being made long before the era of photography, when people wanted a physical reminder of the departed. Jewellery made from the hair of a loved one was the perfect way to keep them close.'

Jewellery made with black enamel or jet, which is in fact fossilised wood, was all that was permitted in the strictly regarded times of mourning following a death in the

1800s. Prince Albert's death inspired a major trade in jet that flourished in Whitby, North Yorkshire, where it occurred in abundance.

Black wasn't the only colour used in mourning jewellery, with white enamel signifying the death of a virgin and pearls, a child. Typically, it was brooches, lockets and rings that were made in memory of a loved one.

Before the Prince's untimely death, there were other fashions associated with the Royal Family, as Roo explains. 'Acrostic jewellery was also popular, where the first letter of each gem spelled out a meaningful word. "Dearest" is a good example and may have been spelled out by a diamond, emerald, amethyst, ruby, emerald, sapphire and topaz.

'You may notice some Scottish designs of this era, which were inspired by Victoria and Albert's newly purchased Scottish Balmoral Estate.'

And at the end of the mourning period that had followed Albert's death, there was another phase in jewellery fashion.

'Finally, the Aesthetic period marked a return to light-heartedness with symbols of good luck and good fortune,' says Roo. 'Look for crescents, starbursts, wishbones and animal heads. As a queen heading towards her twilight years, her children shone with their own fashions and style. The Edwardian era followed with delicate, elegant jewellery in place of statement pieces.

'The most wonderful thing about Victorian jewellery is that each piece was a statement, borne out of love and sentiment. Such emotion will forever stay with that piece centuries later.'

Later, one fashion gave way to another, with some jewellery being made with a more cryptic meaning. As women campaigned for equal rights in the face of often violent opposition from a hostile parliament, wealthy supporters wore suffragette jewellery in a gesture of support, as Thomas Forrester, another qualified gemologist, explains.

'Suffragette jewellery was made in three colours; purple for dignity, white for purity and green for hope. The stones used were usually amethyst (for purple), pearl or white enamel (for white) and peridot or demantoid garnets (for green), which are rare.'

It seems likely that, before long, fashion trumped the political meaning of the jewellery. However, a code attached to jewels is as old as time, says Thomas.

'Centuries ago, amber − fossilised tree resin − was plucked off the beach and since then, it's been associated with the power of the sun.

'Pliny the Elder talked about precious stones in his book, *The Natural History*, which reveals how they were interpreted in the first century. And since then, gems have been given various attributes; lapis lazuli is among those linked to communication, and jade to wisdom.'

Jewellery from Victorian and Edwardian times was handmade by craftsmen and *Bargain Hunt's* Ben Cooper's ancestors were among them. His great grandfather, Charles Smith, a skilled jewellery maker, joined with cousin and investor Edwin Pepper to open a factory in Birmingham in 1899. The choice of the Midlands' city was key to its success, as Ben explains.

'In London, the jewellery makers belonged to ancient guilds, with associated costs. Birmingham was a free city and, with the Industrial Revolution, it became known as the city of 1,001 trades.'

The Smith & Pepper factory was in the heart of the Jewellery Quarter and became particularly famous for the bangles produced there. The so-called 'bamboo' snap-on bangles were enduringly popular, as were serpent-themed bracelets, fashionable after the treasures of Tutankhamen were discovered in the early twenties. The head of the serpent gripping its own tail was also a symbol of fidelity.

Charles had nine children, with his eldest son Eric taking over the business, assisted by siblings Tom and Olive.

As a child, Ben and his brothers were frequent visitors to the factory and he watched spellbound as his great uncle Tom smelted gold. There were cries of amazement from the youngsters as small coins were flattened in the rollers used to iron out thin sheets of precious metals. By then there was some level of automation in the factory, in terms of punching out shapes, but for most of the factory's history, it was workers with hacksaws and handheld drills, peering through magnifying glasses, that produced the most sought-after items. (It was quite a way through a seven year apprenticeship before workers were permitted to wield tools.)

Ben was fascinated by what he saw. 'When you look inside a ring made then, the workmanship at the back is as beautiful as the front. When it was made it went through the hands of several craftsmen, responsible for making, finishing and polishing it.'

For Ben, jewellery made in this era will always be superior in construction to modern equivalents.

'Cast-made pieces have stones cut to precisely the same size. There's real individuality to a handmade piece. You know that none of the stones in the setting are going to be the same.

'This isn't just a case of hankering after the past. With the pressure on speed and price with modern, mass-manufactured jewellery, the artistry has gone.'

When the doors of the Smith & Pepper factory were locked for the last time, its work benches and belt-driven machinery lay untouched for years before being transformed into the Museum of the Jewellery Quarter. And happily, a resurgence of interest in hand-crafted jewellery centred on Birmingham has helped revive an interest in the craftsmanship skills at risk of disappearing in the modern world.

GOLD

Thanks to its hallmarks, gold rises above its imitators but, as a buyer, there are still issues to be settled and personal choice is key.

The purest form of gold is measured at 24 carats. Naturally yellow in colour, it's not used for jewellery because it's so soft. So, the highest value gold likely to be found in wedding bands, for example, is 22 carats.

Next comes 18-carat gold, which is three-quarters gold, with the rest comprising metal alloys. Beyond that is 14 carats, coming in at 58.8 per cent pure gold, which was popular with Victorian and Edwardian craftsmen. Nine carat has the lowest purity ratio. Being just 37.5 per cent gold, it is considerably cheaper than the rest, but is also the most appropriate for jewellery as it is such a durable form of this precious metal. It's the hallmark rather than the colour that is significant as the alloys that are mixed in can change its hue, with copper being added to produce rose gold, for example.

Always check the hallmarks carefully before making any purchases, as an 18-carat item is worth more than something made from 9-carat gold.

KEEP IT CLEAN

If you suspect there's a hidden treasure in your jewellery box but it's covered with the muck of ages, what can you do? With any luck, it will be diamonds encrusted with grime as they are the most straightforward gem to clean. Use baby soap and a soft toothbrush. However, bear in mind that emeralds are porous, rubies can fracture and unloved opals have a habit of falling out of their ring settings. With any stones other than diamonds, it's best to let a professional do the clean-up.

Buying jewellery at antiques fairs can be a minefield, as great age is no guarantee of popularity. With swiftly changing fashions, bear these points in mind:

1. Brooches are deemed largely unfashionable these days, although themed ones, like specific animals, may retain some appeal. Check the history of brooch clasps if you need help to date one.

2. Still, gem clusters are timeless, whether they are rings, earrings or brooches. Queen Victoria wore them, as did Princess Diana. Her engagement ring, consisting of a 12-carat oval blue sapphire,

surrounded by fourteen solitaire diamonds in an 18-carat white gold setting has passed to Kate, Duchess of Cambridge. When it comes to jewellery, the Royal Family often sets trends that others follow.

3. Beautifully made items from the Arts and Crafts movement, loosely between about 1880 and 1920, usually attract a lot of interest at auction.

4. Scandanavian silver has ridden a wave of popularity for a while and items designed by David Andersen have terrific currency. One of his sterling silver bracelets with links of red enamel leaves, bought for £100 by a *Bargain Hunt* team, sold at auction for £120.

Think of jewellery and it's surely diamonds, pearls, gold, silver and precious stones that come to mind. Yet, one jewellery designer left her mark by choosing plastic as her medium. Lea Stein was born in Paris in 1931 and married a chemist, Fernand Steinberger. Together they learned how to layer and laminate thin layers of celluloid acetate, which would be baked for long periods before being cut into shapes. The result was a series of brooches that were quirky, stylish and colourful. Animals were a frequent theme, but she also produced an array of other subjects that could be distinguished not only by the evident painstaking quality but also by the artist's name on a distinctive V-shaped clasp.

A tray of bright brooches caught the eye of one *Bargain Hunt* team, who were immediately advised by their expert, Tim Weeks, that they were reproductions, in the style of Lea Stein, as there was no signature on the brooch pin. 'We are comfortable with that, as long as the price is right, as each Lea Stein brooch would go for between £30 and £60,' advised Tim. Although the brooches were £5 each, the team managed to get a selection of four for just £10. And when it came to auction, they sold for £140, making a 1,300 per cent profit.

Analyse That: Materials and Medium

In the second step in his guide to valuation for beginners, John Cameron browses through the substance of an object under scrutiny, and the clues it might provide.

'Through the centuries, the materials used in the production of both functional and decorative things have changed. Some for natural or ecological reasons, some for political or social reasons and some simply as a result of trial and error. For example, the process of electroplating base metals with a fine layer of silver was first developed on a commercial scale during the 1840s, first by George Elkington in Britain and also licensed to Charles Christofle of France. From this date, we see a huge amount of cheaper electroplated tableware across Europe.

'The materials used in the production of an item can be a useful guide to age, country of origin, maker and quality. Illustrated books and photographs can provide a visual guide to the basic identification but there really is no substitute for the physical handling of things to be really sure of what materials they are made from. Having a basic knowledge of when different materials were first used, became scarce, went out of fashion or came back in fashion will prove, time and time again, a useful indicator to other pieces of the jigsaw.'

First time at an auction? Here are some tips to get you started

1. Auction houses pride themselves on having something for everyone. You can look up the nearest one to you online and discover what's coming up. Check out the catalogues beforehand to find out which lots interest you most.

2. On *Bargain Hunt*, sellers fees aren't deducted from the teams' profits – or losses – but usually they are incurred by anyone who buys or sells at an auction, so find out what they are before bidding. Then there's VAT to consider, and the cost of removing large items. Acquaint yourself with all the likely charges beforehand. Don't get confused between high street auction houses and internet sites that run online against-the-clock auctions. Always read the conditions

of sale as they vary between salerooms and bear in mind BH expert and auctioneer Colin Young's mantra: 'Bid, pay, take it away. Never make it more complicated than that.'

3. If you want to attend an auction then it is best to inform the auction house to tell them you are coming. Personal preferences might keep you at home and there are several large internet sites commonly used by auctioneers that will allow you to bid remotely. However, says JP, most charge for the service, so check if the auction house has its own internet platform, which is likely to be free, and use that instead.

4. Attend the viewing day that precedes an auction. See and handle as many items as you can as, says Kate Bliss, this is a tactile business. Presenter Charlie Ross concurs. 'Although you can read about history, you really have to handle items to properly learn about them. You will most likely feel a chip or a crack in a vase or a dink in a silver box if it's at your fingertips. If it's a chair, sit in it; if it's a piece of jewellery, try it on,' he says.

5. If you can't get to the viewing, ask for a condition report on specific items of interest

from the auction house. It's an honest opinion, freely given. That way, as Tim Weeks points out, you can bid with absolute confidence.

6. Check the results of previous auctions, which will indicate the likely value of an object.

7. 'Don't be shy,' says Tim Weeks. Turn up on time. Walk into the room confidently.

8. Set yourself a budget for the buys you have in your sights. If your target is an item that often comes up for sale, there's no point paying a high price should a bidding war break out. Equally, if it's a rarity that's exactly right for your lounge, and something you've been seeking for years, cut yourself some slack or risk regret when the highest bidder walks away with it – and it's not you.

9. It's a myth to think you might inadvertently purchase a multi-thousand-pound picture by scratching your nose. Auctioneers are savvy enough to sort a genuine bid from a bodily tic. So put that worry to one side and enjoy the day.

3

TOYS

The story of toys is one that mostly belongs to the twentieth century. Certainly, there's evidence children played sport and games in ancient times. Much later, when Queen Victoria was on the throne, there was a narrow spectrum of choice with which youngsters could flex their imaginations. At home, Bible stories inspired the creation of Noah's Arks, inhabited by carved animals, while snakes and ladders was a popular game. There were pull-along models, puppets and wooden dolls for a fortunate few. Outside, children played with spinning tops, cups and hoops and jacks. Yet most children had no time for toys, as they were working all hours in factories or fields.

As the twentieth century dawned, there came a voracious appetite for toys, driven by a new age of mass manufacturing coupled with a growing desire to give children a childhood. Today, there are countless collectors, and they are not just looking for rudimentary Edwardian toys either.

Bargain Hunt's Tim Weeks is not only an auctioneer and an expert but an enthusiast himself, and he says that toys are top of the lots in auctions right now. There is, he explains, a twenty-five-year cycle that informs what is going to be the next big thing.

'You never forget the toys that had an impact on you in childhood,' he explains. 'These are toys you may have been given with that "wow" factor on Christmas morning, or toys your friends had that you wished you'd had.

'Children become teenagers when they are no longer interested in the toys they once played with avidly. But as adults, they become nostalgic for those childhood days and they have a bit more disposable income in their pockets. That's when they start to buy back the toys they played with when they were children.'

Of course, the hot trends change with every decade. Back in 1985, Transformers – with their multiple moving parts – burst onto the scene, eclipsing Care Bears and Cabbage Patch dolls with their popularity. Optimus Prime was broadly considered the elite of the range.

A little over a decade later, children were transfixed by Pixar's *Toy Story* and Buzz Lightyear figures were the most sought-after toy – and consequently were in short supply.

When Tim was young, *Teenage Mutant Hero Turtles* were the best-loved cartoons on Saturday morning television and later the turtles manifested themselves into toy figures. In fact, Tim missed most episodes and was bitterly resentful about it as he explains.

'My dad was an auctioneer and, aged nine, I would be taken to his saleroom where, to me, he would be selling what I considered to be old rubbish when I wanted to be at home watching cartoons, like my friends. I thought it was the worst job in the world.

'But within a few years, I had already decided I wanted to become an auctioneer. Now I think I have the best job in the world. I love the items I sell, I love the people I'm selling to and I love the element of performance at the rostrum.'

The game-changing franchise for toy collectors was *Star Wars*, which first steam-rollered into cinemas in 1977.

'The *Star Wars* films have been extremely successful,' says Tim. 'But sales of the toys linked to the series outperform the movies.'

Recent rostrum results prove his point. A rare rocket-firing Boba Fett figure sold for £18,600 in 2021. It was among 700 items amassed by a French collector since childhood.

It's always worth rooting around any toy box that's been retired to the loft to search for undiscovered gems. After all, rare toys are often more common finds than, say, antique gold watches. But it's unlikely that's where the big money figurines will be found, as Tim explains.

'Millions of *Star Wars* figures were made all over the world. The packaging was ripped open within five minutes of going through the checkout.

'What today's collectors are looking for are unopened toys that never went to the shop floor. These figures have not even made it out of the warehouse or the stockroom.'

The most valuable will be those in 'unpunched' packaging, that is, the hole at the top of the cardboard backing, usually poked through by the prongs on display units, remains in position. Beyond that, even a dink in the protective plastic window that surrounds the toy can cost an owner hard cash at auction.

If the packaging is long gone, tiny plastic accessories – the sort that normally disappear up the vacuum cleaner – may still enhance the value of a figure in a saleroom. The Hammer of Thundera, a small but distinctive weapon wielded by Thundercat Bengali, will be worth more than any Thundercat figure you care to mention, says Tim. In 1970, a martial arts Action Man was released with seven different coloured belts, and it is the short, narrow pieces of fabric that are worth considerably more than the figure they decorated. Forty years later, a similar figure was released, distinguished by having lighter coloured stitching on the white judo suit, with only three belts – an entirely different prospect for collectors and not nearly as desirable as the original.

It's not just handheld toys that adults recall with fondness, but the electronic games they played at a time when technology was in its infancy. Some had to be hooked up to the television, and most were chunky, out-sized versions of those that exist today, including mobile phones that even then were derisively called 'bricks'. The first, best-known computer game was Pong, made by Atari for arcades before 1975, which was produced for home use through television sets. Two opposing players each operated an on-screen, paddle which propelled an on-screen ball. According to Tim, they are antiques of the future that are collectible today – and it's not just the consoles but the games cartridges that can attract cash interest. Still, always keep this short guide in mind:

1. Condition is key.
2. If you are buying, look for boxed, near-mint condition.
3. If you are selling, keep all paperwork and instructions intact to garner the best prices.

Other crazes that swept the nation are also putting in a strong performance at auction houses and Pokémon cards, launched in Japan in 1996, have had an enormous impact. Taking the company's 'Gotta Catch 'Em All' slogan to heart, many children used their pocket money to purchase cards featuring characters like Zoroark, Victini and Volcanion.

Twenty-five years after the craze gripped the nation, a single card (Dark Charizard) was sold for £4,600 in an auction in Staffordshire, which also had an unopened base set booster box that sold for £16,000.

The previous year in America, another Charizard card was sold for more than $220,000 (£174,000). The purchaser was rap star Logic, who confessed to a lifelong Pokémon passion. Afterwards, Logic – real name Sir Robert Bryson Hall IL – said: 'I remember even trying to trade food stamps for [Pokémon] cards, and now . . . as a grown man, it's like buying back a piece of something I could never have. It's not about the material, it's about the experience.'

If the unyielding surfaces of plastic figures and sticky playing cards do nothing for you, it may be more appropriate to look further back in time, at toys that your grandparents might recognise.

These stuffed toys were named for the US president Theodore Roosevelt, after he apparently spared a bear on a hunting expedition in 1902, and they launched a toy craze like no other. The most famous maker of the era was Margarete Steiff, a seamstress in a factory in Germany and already a successful stuffed toy maker. When an American saw her range of bears at the Leipzig Fair in 1903, he snapped up supplies. *Bargain Hunt's* Roo Irvine takes up the story.

'Margarete was self-taught, despite being confined to a wheelchair due to polio. In the 1870s, aged 30, she founded her own company, making felt clothing and toy animals.

'By 1906, she had 2,200 employees to meet the ferocious demand for teddy bears, and their greatest year for teddy bear sales was 1907 when they sold 975,000 bears. Other companies tried to compete, but Steiff had cornered the market first, and reaped the rewards.'

Steiff bears were distinctive for having humped backs, long snouts, large tapered feet and elongated arms with pads made from felt, and it's these bear-like features that collectors seek today. From 1904, Steiff bears could also be distinguished by the button sewn in their ears. A decade later, boot button eyes were replaced with glass ones and the original wood wool stuffing was superseded by another dense natural fibre, kapok.

German-made bears disappeared from toy shop shelves during the First World War, with replacements in this era of shortages made from army coats, shirts and blankets. British companies stepped up and in 1921 it was a bear from J. K. Farnell that became the inspiration for *Winnie the Pooh*. Merrythought, a Shropshire-based company, then developed the broad-headed, wide-eared bear. Manufacturers developed trademarks in the way noses were sewn and limbs were shaped. Nylon silk plush became the fabric of choice for bodies after 1938, while wartime bears were filled with 'sub', in essence the sweepings from the mill floor. Thankfully, in the 1950s, when foam replaced sub as stuffing and bears were finally made from a single piece of material rather than being jointed, the toys became washable. New child safety devices had plastic noses attached to bears' faces and screw-in plastic eyes replacing glass.

Older teddies – and other stuffed animals made by companies like Steiff, including dogs, cats and elephants – can still be worth money at auction, but there's lots to discover before putting any childhood pal under the hammer.

Roo elaborates: 'The collectible teddy bear market is so niche that to truly appreciate the value of what you have, requires thorough research. Everything from the shape of the nose, colour of the eyes and positioning of the ears is crucial in identification of the company, era and model!'

Meanwhile, being cherished for decades by an owner is both a weakness and a strength. A great sentimental bond means a bear will survive for decades, or even generations. However, relentless cuddling puts its plush body at risk and being well-loved can knock down the value of elderly teddies considerably. Even teddies in good condition can fail to capture hearts at the auction. A vintage Chad Valley bear, made several decades ago in England was bought by Kate Bliss for her bonus buy. She paid £18, but it only managed a hammer price of £15 despite looking almost new.

Replica twentieth-century teddies are now widely available, but be wary, advises Tim Weeks.

'Buy them and enjoy them; that is their value. Don't invest in contemporary bears because, like second-hand cars, they will likely halve in value once they leave the saleroom.'

There's another financial health warning over puzzles and games, which are unlikely to ever achieve a high resale price because pieces are so easily lost. However, that's not the same for model trains.

The first mass-market train sets were made by a German company called Märklin in 1891. It was the golden age of steam trains in Britain and everyone wanted a stake in the action. Thanks to innovator Wenman Bassett-Lowke, it was possible for affluent British people to at least purchase miniature versions of famous locomotives after he imported Märklin models and modified them. With hostility to Germany running high after the First World War, he started factories of his own.

Ultimately, it was Frank Hornby who made train sets more accessible to young people. His was a story in two parts. Hornby created something he first dubbed 'Mechanics Made Easy' at the turn of the twentieth century because he was disappointed with the creative options available in the toy market. For children who liked construction, the metal kits hit the mark and were a huge success at the time, although Meccano, as it became known, does not hold the same broad appeal today. A box of assorted Meccano pieces bought by one *Bargain Hunt* team for £165 sold for just £45, leaving a painful loss of £120.

Hornby used the money he had made through the creation of Meccano to produce books, tracks, scenery and, of course, trains, for play. He had even introduced electric layouts by the 1930s. By the early 1950s, model trains were among the most popular Christmas toys and, like Meccano, there were always additions on sale for Hornby train sets.

Happily, trains have had a more enduring appeal than Meccano and are sound antique fair buys, says Tim. Not only do they appeal to those with a working layout in their lofts, but also to collectors of railway memorabilia.

ROCKING HORSES

Train sets are not the only traditional toys that enjoy longevity and another in the stable, rocking horses, are also perennial favourites. But Bargain Hunt teams usually find these mighty beasts outside their budgets, even when the horses are relatively recently made. The natural successors of hobby horses, they became particularly popular among the wealthy in Victorian times and were painted dapple grey, to reflect the Queen's personal preferences. Riders often took a tumble from early models, which were hefty and precariously perched on rockers. Later, lighter hollow models were manufactured, astride the swinger or safety stand patented by a US designer in the 1880s.

One *Bargain Hunt* team fell for a modern version and happily paid £59, but at auction the wooden horse sold for just £30, meaning a £29 loss.

To make a profit, look for a bit of age and preferably a maker's mark that denotes a high-quality manufacturer from the Victorian period. Those names include F H Ayres and G & J Lines, both London-based, J Collinson of Liverpool, Swan Toys of Leeds and Brassington & Cooke in Manchester.

MODEL CARS

Another toy from the past that's always popular is the die-cast model car.

Dinky – part of Hornby's toy empire – were the first to produce a line in the 1930s. After the war came Lesney, manufacturers of a Coronation coach replica, then Corgi, who took the market by storm by putting plastic windows on their models. By the 1960s, it proved a lucrative market and Matchbox, the latest, biggest brand, was turning out a million per week. More durable than today's equivalents, there's a robust market for re-sale. As always, boxed models, or those in exceptional condition, command the highest prices. However, be warned that the boxes themselves can be forged as new versions of old packaging have been produced to capitalise on prices. Imposter boxes stand out for their brighter print colours and lack of damage. Also, an old box always bears a musty smell, as a tribute to its great age. A new one simply smells of cardboard. No matter how pristine, an original box will bear some patina and, with a bit of luck, a pencilled on price in shillings and pence. Most examples of cars were handheld and hand-hurled, so are also likely to bear some evidence of wear, but that doesn't necessarily mean they won't be profitable.

One *Bargain Hunt* team bought up a box of toy cars for £25, which sold at auction for £48, nearly doubling their money. Buying in quantity often brings a healthy discount and appeals to bidders who feel they have a chance of discovering a rare model.

Overlooked and Undervalued

Tim advocates rummaging around collections of toy cars and advises buyers to look for the

Tri-ang Spot-On models, as these are harder to come by, so are more sought after by collectors – and you might pick one up inexpensively.

Tri-ang also made much larger pedal cars and one made from sheet metal, dating from the 1960s, caught the attention of one *Bargain Hunt* team. Their expert, Chuko Ojiri, also admired the model, which had undergone some sympathetic restoration work but still had the original dashboard. A negotiated price of £148 still felt like a risk, but at auction the car made £210, making a £62 profit.

DOLLS

Still further back in time came porcelain dolls, made from the mid-1800s and generally far too fragile for play. The porcelain and its shiny, glazed surface was soon replaced with bisque, a matt alternative that gave a more realistic skin tone. Many have undergone repairs for cosmetic purposes. Even from their earliest incarnation, these dolls became collectors' items, but today only the rare, perfect examples are sought after at auction. You can tell if a porcelain doll's head has been repaired by holding it up to the light. The outline of any work carried out on it will be reflected back at you. An unrepaired doll will also give the same clear ring as a china cup when it is tapped, rather than a dull thud.

UNUSUAL TOYS

Quirky toys are always popular at auction, as one team that purchased a remote-controlled racing car in its box discovered. The pair paid £30 for the car, which sold for £50 at auction. Hoping to cash in on a similar sentiment, another *Bargain Hunt* team paid £34 for a Japanese-made robot. But the faith they placed in the idiosyncratic toy was shattered when it sold at auction for only £25. Although their conviction that toys like these were collectible was a sound one, they were wide of the mark with this one. The key is the date of robot toys, with models dating from the sixties much more valuable than the one from the eighties that they had snapped up. Tin-plate space toys are also more likely to attract attention than plastic ones. Bought by one *Bargain Hunt* team for £57.50, one tin-plate space rocket soared to an auction price of £110, yielding a healthy profit of £52.50.

TOY SOLDIERS

Small but perfectly formed, toy soldiers have been relished by children down the decades. Once produced to help military bigwigs plan their next strategy, their numbers bloomed after 1893 when toy maker William Britain found a way to make hollow, cast-lead soldiers, making them lighter and more affordable than ever before. The height of 2.25 inches (57 millimetres) – is now the industry standard. As war was an overarching feature of the first half of the twentieth century, these diminutive military men were a sure-fire hit and lead soldiers in British and foreign uniforms became the toys that fired the imagination of children everywhere, including Winston Churchill and novelist H.G. Wells.

There were changes afoot after the Second World War, as plastic became more popular. The arrival of the new medium, coupled with legislation concerning lead's safety passed in 1966, meant the manufacture of heavy-metal soldiers was dispatched to history. But even plastic soldiers retain some draw for collectors, who generally want sets of everything. And throughout the history of toy soldiers, there has been no limit to the sets available, extending from British regiments to Foreign Legion fighters through to cowboys and spacemen. As well as Britains, popular manufacturers include Marx, Timpo, Minikins and John Hill & Co.

Pristine toy soldiers in their original packages can still attract high prices, even at a time when the appetite for them has dimmed. *Bargain Hunt's* Richard Madley has good reason to recall the set of lead soldiers he was given as a boy.

'It was every young boy's dream to wake up on Christmas morning to find a cardboard box full of Britains' lead soldiers of a particular regiment. They were so loved the soldiers soon became play worn, so when they did survive, they became quite collectible, with the 1930s being a heyday.'

However, he explains, after plastic took over as the toy fabric of choice, he was disappointed after being presented with a boxed set of lead soldiers by his father. Richard thought the soldiers old-fashioned and clunky and, confronted by this evident frustration, his father – an auctioneer – gave him some sound advice: to put the box away unopened. Years later, Richard himself sold it at auction and raised enough money to put a new roof on his home. Prices have since tumbled, he concedes, but the fabulous condition of the soldiers in their unhandled box ensured that they would command a premium price. (At a similar time, he sold his postcard collection accrued over years and raised enough money for a central heating system, while his wife sold the vesta cases she had been collecting since she was a child to buy a new kitchen.)

Twentieth-century Toys and Games Timeline: Discover the Decade in which your Favourite Toys First Appeared

1900–1910: Teddy bears, Plasticine, crayons, pedal cars, Meccano

1911–1920: Mass-produced marbles, Hornby train sets

1921–1930: Electric model trains, Mickey Mouse, mass-produced yo-yos

1931–1940: Scrabble, Monopoly, die-cast model cars

1941–1950: Slinky, Lego

1951–1960: Mr Potato Head, Scalextric, Barbie, Sindy, skateboards

1961–1970: Etch A Sketch, stylophones, Thunderbirds, Action Man, Twister, Spirograph, Rubik's Cube

1971–1980: Space Hopper, Magna Doodle, Uno, Pong, *Star Wars* toys, Lego Space, Trivial Pursuit

1981–1990: BMX bikes, My Little Pony, Care Bears, Transformers, Sylvanian Families, Game Boy, Teenage Mutant Hero Turtles

1991–2000: Thunderbirds (again), Pokémon, Power Rangers, POGS, *Toy Story* characters, Beanie Babies, Teletubbies, Tamagotchi, Furby

Analyse That: Object Identification and Form

Every item heading for auction needs a catalogue description, so it's a good idea to learn about long-lost items from our collective past. John Cameron shares some of the lessons he has learned.

'When I first worked part-time in an auction house to supplement my college studies, I was amazed at the number of items, especially those used in formal/dining rooms, I had never heard of before. Through the centuries, our social standards and living habits have undergone a continual evolution. The effect tea, or rather its importation, had across Europe in the early eighteenth century, especially on the development of functional items used in the tea-drinking ceremony, is a good example to cite. When tea was first imported into Europe in the latter half of the seventeenth century, it was an extremely expensive commodity that only the upper classes could afford in any quantity. Teapots, first made in Europe of silver and later pottery and porcelain, became desirable status symbols in wealthy homes during the early 1700s, as did lockable wooden tea caddies and silver caddy spoons, yet these items were unknown a century before, except in the Far and Middle East. Today, as most people make tea with teabags, tea caddies and caddy spoons are redundant, except as decorative items. This then, is where a sound knowledge of history, especially social history, will pay dividends. The form or shape, like the object and the materials from which it is made, will be an indication to age as, like fashion, it will evolve or alter over time.

'Being able to identify items with confidence will only come with experience, or plenty of study and cross-reference. This is where reading annual price guides can be used to good effect and I confess that it was looking through my grandfather's books, aged ten, that first fostered my interest. Looking at pictures and absorbing the descriptions, or the key words, and cross-referencing unfamiliar words with a decorative arts dictionary is an enjoyable and easy way to learn. Most specialist reference books and collector's guides contain a useful "glossary of terms" section at the back, sometimes accompanied by illustrations.'

4

TRAVEL

Summer holidays, city breaks and ski seasons are all firmly established features of modern life. So, it follows that the rich history of travel and tourism impacts on the antiques we cherish and the mementoes in our homes.

For thousands of years, people have traversed the globe in search of power and resources. It's why Roman coins are dug up in British fields with surprising regularity. The Spilsby Hoard is one such example. Containing 281 coins produced by Roman mints in Europe, it was uncovered by two detectorists in Lincolnshire in 2014. The coins were sold three years later for £600.

After conquest and trade, the next historical prompt for travel was religion, with countless thousands undertaking pilgrimages at home and abroad during the Middle Ages and beyond. They travelled huge distances to see religious relics, including bones, blood and, more commonly, wood and nails purporting to be from Jesus' crucifix. At shrines, each pilgrim was given a metal badge to prove he had visited, and these are still being uncovered today.

After King Henry VIII broke away from the Catholic church the number of pilgrimages declined. But investment in exploration accelerated as merchants had the unexploited wealth of new territories within their sights. In 1600 the East India Company was incorporated, which contrived a monopoly on British trade routes with the East. As its tentacles spread, so the company acted more like a conquering power than a trading partner. Its strong-armed approach across the Indian subcontinent, China and Southeast Asia transformed the range of imports to Britain, and most aristocratic homes bore the hallmarks of company activity, in the form of plush fabrics, ornate porcelain and eye-catching gems.

Tales from the Auction House

On a valuer visit, Nick Hall's eye was caught by
a six-foot-tall metal goddess Guan Yin standing
in a hallway. With its thousand hands and
imposing height it was, he felt sure, a centuries-
old statue of the revered Buddhist Goddess of
Mercy, probably from a temple in China.
Although the owner had been told by other
auction houses it was a nineteenth-century
replica, Nick started investigating. After
recruiting an expert in Chinese metalwork to
scrutinise the item, Nick discovered there was a
similar one in the British Museum. It dated from
the late Ming dynasty and was worth at least
£50,000. When it finally went under the
hammer, the price was £126,000 – and the
buyer, who was Chinese, wanted to repatriate it.
Later, Nick tracked the route of the statue from

China to Britain and discovered that, years before, it had come from the home of a British diplomat and had been originally sold in a rural auction held after his death.

Perhaps the first example of foreign travel for its own sake comes in the form of the Grand Tour, a trans-European trip for those who were young and wealthy in an era that started in about 1660 – although the word 'tourist' didn't come into common parlance until 1772. Itineraries were weighted with artistic and academic pursuits, and the route from Britain was through France and Switzerland to Italy, with the return journeys made through Germany and the Netherlands. After the Channel crossing, the mode of transport was usually coach, and sometimes ship, as travellers, attended by a retinue of servants, sought to immerse themselves in different cultures. They took with them letters of introduction, which effectively acted as credit notes. Before returning home, they bought carved marbles, cast bronzes, art and glass as mementoes. The age of the Grand Tour ended in the middle of the nineteenth century at the same time the era of tourism began in earnest.

There were several strands to this new travel epoch, rooted in the Industrial Revolution. Firstly, there was an improving distribution of wealth, with the middle classes being created through the proliferation of industry. And even working people eventually had enough money in their pockets to spend on leisure pursuits. Then came the age of steam.

While rails had been in use, on and off, for centuries, an engine to ride on them wasn't unveiled until the early nineteenth century, when industrial static steam engines were superseded by moving ones that hauled people rather than coal. Networks rapidly mushroomed around Britain and Europe. Soon, trains were achieving mighty speeds and travellers were transported for longer distances, in shorter time frames than ever before, while companies competed to bring prices down. With the institution of bank holidays in 1871, the notion of the long weekend was forged.

With one eye on this changing landscape in the new age of the train, Thomas Cook stepped up in 1841 to run his first organised outing. It started small. Cook arranged a modest train trip between Leicester and Loughborough on behalf of the Temperance Movement, advocating against alcohol. Some 500 working people turned up at the station and for most it was their first experience of a steam railway. The trip got underway with plenty of flag waving, cheering and even the presence of a brass band. The one shilling ticket price included afternoon tea as well.

Today, vintage trains have a veritable army of fans, many of which will be stoked at the sight of steam railway paraphernalia. One Bargain Hunt team was depending on it after buying a cast-iron plate from a railway company. The plate bore both the name of the London and North Eastern Railway and the city of Darlington. Formed in 1923, the company had a short, illustrious history before railway nationalisation in 1948. However, as well as running prestigious high-speed trains along 6,500 miles of track under its control, it hauled coal from the collieries of the North East. The chunky plate, bought for £25, sold for £65, justifying the team's decision to buy an industrial item rather than a decorative one.

Steam impacted travel on the high seas as well as on land. Sail had been used to power ships for centuries, but duly gave way to steam and, before the age of the train, people had travelled around Britain on coasters, enjoying considerably more comfort than the alternative, an overland coach. A web of canals built just prior to the Industrial era helped with navigation. Indeed, the first seagoing steam ship travelled between Leeds and Yarmouth in 1813. This was just the start and a quarter of a century later, Isambard Kingdom Brunel ushered in the age of transatlantic crossings with the maiden voyage of the SS Great Western. While some used the upper decks of this new generation of shipping for leisure, many were travelling in steerage; immigrants searching for a new life with better prospects, or to escape persecution.

Cruise liner decks were typically strewn with chairs for passengers to enjoy the vista during the voyage and it was a rattan recliner that inspired expert Gary Pe on one *Bargain Hunt*. Although his team were unsure, the fold-down chair and stool – a predecessor of the deckchair – was reminiscent of seats his father used while travelling by ship. With nailed-on provenance, a chair such as this might make reasonable money. One plucked from the ocean after the *Titanic* sank in 1912 was sold at auction in 2015 for £100,000. But the chair that Gary championed had no known history. Auctioneer Catherine Southon pointed out that it did have live woodworm, as well as a burn mark. Although the team spent £78 on the chair, it raised just £10 at auction.

Tales from the Auction House

When auctioneer Charles Hanson started rummaging in a bag containing items destined for a charity shop one item captured his attention. He pulled out a small, patterned jug, the sort he'd previously only read about, and wondered, could this gem with its glorious history really be languishing in the Midlands. He'd identified a ewer that came from an eighteenth-century Chinese emperor's court, not least from the Imperial yellow shade of its body. The quality of craftsmanship on the item, made from copper and covered with enamel, highlighted that the emperor concerned, Qian Long, was a patron of the arts. It was, Charles thought, sacred, important and rare. Only three examples were known when he found it: one in Taiwan, one in Beijing and this, the third, in Burton on Trent. It had been left languishing in a loft by the owner, whose grandfather had travelled in the Far East. The winning auction bid was for £390,000.

For those that couldn't afford tickets for a lengthy rail trip or a cruise, there was another way of getting around: the bicycle – far less grand but with a band of enthusiastic early adopters. Before long, the bicycle became an accepted form of transport for men and women, expanding the horizons of those who could afford to have one. The roots of its inception are cloaked in doubt and may extend back to the time of Leonardo da Vinci, but in more modern times, it morphed from a velocipede to a bone shaker, then a penny-farthing to a 'Rover'. Riding a bicycle got considerably more comfortable with the advent of pneumatic tyres and gears in the closing years of the nineteenth century. Technology had made bicycles sufficiently comfortable and agile for the first Tour de France to be staged in 1903.

An early bicycle was an impulsive buy for one member of a *Bargain Hunt* team, who agreed to buy it for £250 without consulting either his partner or his expert, Stephanie Connell. It was dubbed a butcher's bike as it had a basket on the front, much as a delivery boy would have had in days gone by. But it also had a new saddle, lights, pedals and other improvements, which might by some people's judgement have taken it out of the realm of an original antique. But the buyer had the last laugh. When bidding finally came to a halt, it had reached £320, making a chunky £70 profit.

The twentieth century brought with it motoring and manned flight, two other ways of transporting people to new destinations.

The number of cars on the roads in Britain in 1926 amounted to 1,715,000, revealing the huge potential for day trips even then. Victorian seaside towns were now within reach for increasing numbers, while holiday camps like those launched by Billy Butlins and Harry Warner, which opened in the mid-thirties, were also popular destinations. From 1938, the law made sure everyone had one week's paid holiday a year, enhancing the opportunities for people to take a break. By 1997, the volume of cars on the roads had boomed to 26,974,000 and domestic journeys across the nation were commonplace.

As for flights, the two world wars dented the economic opportunities attached to this mode of transport, but in 1950 the first Horizon Holidays inclusive trips to Corsica got underway. The following year, one million Britons travelled abroad.

It took a few more decades for long haul to become established, taking people further than ever before in their leisure time. The success of the tourism industry lay not only in education and broadening people's outlooks, but in driving a new economic model, the products of which started to line people's mantelpieces or even filled their wardrobes.

Mauchline ware is one such example. Mauchline is a town in southwest Scotland, associated with poet Robbie Burns, that gave its name to an array of wooden souvenirs that sold in quantity to nineteenth-century visitors. Typically, each box or brush was adorned with a transfer decoration of a famous landmark, then varnished. When its popularity was established, the makers expanded to embrace other views and country homes from across Britain. Mauchline ware was also used for manufacturers of stationery or sewing kits, so it spread widely at home and abroad.

A regular find for *Bargain Hunt* teams, a piece of Mauchline ware bought for £10 was sold at auction for £40, reflecting the abiding keenness among collectors.

Another recurring feature of *Bargain Hunt* trawls at antiques fairs across the country are what's known as Black Forest carvings. Originating from Switzerland rather than Bavaria, they come in the form of bears, eagles, stags, dogs and other animals, and emerged from the detritus of tragedy. From the 1840s, the same potato blight that caused such human devastation in Ireland was also at large in Europe. Swiss authorities encouraged hard-pressed workers to take up carving to sell to tourists visiting the country as part of the Grand Tour.

Today, the most commonly found carvings – bears – sell for about £50. But, says expert and enthusiast Nick Hall, it's those in the most unusual designs and with whimsical expressions that command the best money today. A nutcracker shaped like animal jaws might cost as much as £200. His advice for new collectors is to look for:

1. Quality of carving
2. Condition
3. Rarity of the item

One traveller to a far-flung region brought back a tribal mask that landed in among the trio of buys for one *Bargain Hunt* team. Some items like this are genuinely the workmanship of distant tribes, while others are mass produced for a tourist market. The team paid £60 for it and the mask sold for £230, giving them a £170 profit.

And proof that the seaside resorts are just as popular today as they always have been emerged through another *Bargain Hunt* buy, a waist-height model of an ice cream with a flake in it, once used to make trippers drool. It cost £105 and the team made a cool £55 profit when it sold at auction for £160.

Analyse That: Construction Techniques and Components

Technology and technique have evolved over the centuries, and it can be key to dating and valuing items, as John Cameron points out.

'Whatever the subject – glass, furniture, silverware, pottery or clocks – the techniques employed in their production will, like the forms produced and the materials used, have changed and evolved. An understanding of when and why certain changes occurred is a clue to age. For example, when William of Orange and Queen Mary ascended the English throne from the Netherlands in 1688, they encouraged many designers and craftsmen to migrate with them. Distinctively carved and marquetry veneered cabinets from this period, directly influenced by Dutch fashion and made by migrant Dutch craftsmen, marked a stark transition from the more baroque-influenced carved oak furniture produced by contemporary English craftsmen. You will often find that the dissemination of skills and techniques will follow a historical event, be it political or religious.'

Double Bubble

Anything that sells for twice the price paid, or more, falls into the 'double bubble' category. Sometimes the profits only amount to a few pounds, but it's percentage terms that count here.

1. French-made Art Deco cologne bottle

   £12 paid, £34 sold

2. Small clock with Waterford crystal surround, diamond cut to reflect the light

   £18 paid, £50 sold

3. Autoclave, a metal 'cooker' used in industry, science and medicine to alter temperature and pressure

   £35 paid, £70 sold

4. Podiatry set, containing all its pieces

   £30 paid, £80 sold

5. Rack of copper kitchen utensils

   £12 paid, £25 sold

6. Pair of beehive-design Victorian stamped brass candlesticks

   £9 paid, £30 sold

5

GLASS

Glass plays a key role in all our lives, be it in windows and doors, to hold flowers or fine wine, to reflect our faces or refract the light. In glassware, there's a broad appeal for the show's Bargain Hunters who, when they buy, tend to select from favourite eras from its long history.

Glass has been in evidence from the earliest era of history. Obsidian glass occurs near volcanoes when lava cools quickly and for centuries was used for weapons and tools by the earliest civilisations.

Creating glass was a slow process until the Syrians learned how to use a blow pipe, making it easier and cheaper. This industrial advance was soon incorporated into Roman life, then exported around Europe. After the fall of Rome, it took some time for the industry to achieve that scale of excellence again. In medieval times, Venice became the centre of glass-making excellence and, in turn, the most prosperous city in Europe. That's when the extraordinary dogma of the era came into play, that landed its greatest makers in a gilded cage.

Armed with all manner of privileges to keep them sweet, the craftsmen of Venice were exiled to the island of Murano in the late thirteenth century. The government claimed it was to eliminate the risk of a blaze being sparked by the glassmakers' furnaces inside timber-framed buildings, all huddled at close quarters. Maybe. However, it's more likely the real aim was to keep their techniques secret, as glassmakers were soon forbidden to leave the island's shores.

Even then, the glass they produced wasn't clear like it is today. It wasn't until the middle of the fifteenth century that the Venetians discovered the art of making *cristallo* glass, which was entirely colourless, as well as white *lattimo* glass. Venetian mirrors were also in huge demand.

For *Bargain Hunt* expert Roo Irvine, glass is one of life's riddles. It's made from sand, yet it's transparent. And glass can be pretty tough, although it starts life as a liquid. Still made today, Murano glass holds a special slot in glass-making history and Roo tells us why she is a fan.

'Made from silica, soda, lime and potassium, it melts in a special furnace at a temperature of 1,500˚C to reach a liquid state. Gold or silver foil is often added to the glass mixture, along with minerals such as copper for sparkle, zinc for white colour, cobalt for blue, manganese for violet,' she explains. 'The mixture is then mouth-blown and hand-crafted by master glassmakers using special techniques and basic tools, many of which were developed in the Middle Ages and have changed little since then. This results in unique creations, rich in colour with surreal patterns and shapes, true "works of art".'

Today, Murano glass bears a special trademark as proof of its origin. However, there are many reproduction Murano pieces in circulation, some of which have cropped up on *Bargain Hunt*.

Politics and the plague sparked Venice's decline and bohemia, in Germany, stepped into the breach. However, by now, glassmaking secrets were out.

In the middle of the seventeenth century, Britain's George Ravenscroft achieved a technical triumph after experimenting with lead oxide and flint to produce the enduringly fashionable lead crystal. Little is known about Ravenscroft, a Catholic who posed as an Anglican in religiously intolerant times, but he was a frequent visitor to Venice, where he likely got his inspiration. History may even have credited him as the creator of lead crystal rather than an Italian, who was perhaps truly responsible for it.

By the time King George I came to the throne, lead glass had almost entirely usurped the Venetian version that has previously dominated the market. Most glass makers congregated around coal fields after a law that banned them using wood fires was introduced to counter fears of deforestation.

'If you get a chance, handle a Georgian glass,' Roo urges. 'The stories that glass could tell, the lips that glass touched as they sought a reprieve from life's struggles.

'I adore the imperfections of Georgian glass – the "wonky" stem, the centuries of scratches, the glass so heavy you can throw it at the wall and it still won't break. My first Georgian glass? I slept with it under my pillow and it withstood my grip all night!'

The good news for collectors is that glass became more accessible to ordinary people during Georgian times, so there is still plenty to be found. The bad news is that most dealers now realise the worth of these pieces of handheld history.

As she wanders around antiques fairs with *Bargain Hunt* teams in tow, Roo sometimes spots a Georgian glass among reasonably priced oddments. But more often these days, she's seeing them kept in a cabinet, under lock and key.

Although it's notoriously hard to value a glass, that's not to say it isn't sometimes worth big money. A single glass made by the Beilby family of Newcastle upon Tyne in 1769 sold for £15,250 in June 2021. The Beilby family became famous for fusing enamel onto glass, which was sometimes painted.

In one *Bargain Hunt* episode, presenter Eric Knowles contrasted the appeal of two glasses, both with great age but one worth substantially more than the other. Against expectation, the ale glass engraved with hops and with a decorative stem, dating from 1765, was worth £300, while its smaller, squatter and far less elegant rival was five times more valuable.

The more expensive one was a baluster, getting its name from the chunky bobble in its stem. Specifically, it was a toastmaster's glass, hence its small bowl, and was made in 1720. Its rarity, age and unusual use combined to increase its value. Some Georgian glass is priced more reasonably, although it's worth checking your sideboard shelves in case your Georgian grandfather was a careful drinker!

In Georgian times glasses were made in three parts, with the most junior worker tackling the base, a craftsman producing the decorative stem and the boss making a bowl and eventually forging the three parts together. Georgian glasses have been faked, so here's a quick guide to help you check for authenticity:

1. Make sure the base hasn't been ground down to disguise a chip. Look for the pontil mark, where the pontil rod – used in the glass-blowing process – has

been snapped off after the glass was made. Sometimes it presents like a little nodule, easily felt by a finger.

2. Georgian glasses are usually grey in colour, rather than bright white. One way of identifying Georgian glass is that it looks smoky when you put white paper behind it.

3. When they are pushed together side by side, the feet of Georgian glasses normally touch before the bowls do.

4. Look for bubbles, 'stones' or 'seeds' in Georgian glass. These are likely to be present because of the way the glass was made.

5. Tap the glass edge with your finger. Lead glass will ring for some moments.

6. Expect to see striations, or tiny grooves, on old glasses, imprinted during the manufacturing process.

In 1745, during the reign of George II, a tax was imposed on raw materials used in glassmaking, starting a century of punitive taxation that brought the industry to its knees. But one by-product of that troubled time was the creation of air-filled glass stems, making them lighter and more delicate.

Possibly reflecting the escalating costs of glass, it was also the era of glass rinsers at banquet tables; a modest tub filled with water that diners could use to wash glasses in between the many wine courses. Three Georgian glass rinsers bought by one *Bargain Hunt* team for £38 sold for £60 at auction.

In the same year as the Glass Excise came the Jacobite rebellion, and drinking vessels from the era remain a thrilling find, as Roo explains. The Jacobite rebellion was short-lived, and finally extinguished by defeat at the Battle of Culloden in 1746. Reprisals against the rebels were fierce, and three Jacobite Lords were executed the following year, shortly before all prisoners from the episode were pardoned.

'Jacobean glass is a perfect example of coded symbolism, and one of the rare occasions where the glass you drank from could lead to your own execution.

'The "offending" glass was delicately engraved using small copper wheels by expert wheel-engravers in London during the 1740s. The symbols and motifs that define Jacobean glass were often derived from nature, the white heraldic rose with six petals representing the King, James Stuart. If a rosebud is to the right of the rose, this represents Bonnie Prince Charlie. A rosebud to the left of the Rose represents his younger brother, Prince Henry Benedict Stuart.

'Other symbols that represented the Stuart's claim to the throne were the Thistle, the Prince of Wales's feathers and the acorn and oak leaf.'

Mystery Object

Although it looks like a short, stout glass, there's nowhere to put drink because the indentation at the top is so shallow. Rather than liquid, this was made to hold ice cream sold by street vendors in Victorian times. They were called penny licks and, given the shape of the glass, you didn't get many mouthfuls for your money. But customers often got much more than they bargained for, in the shape of harmful bacteria. It was an age when cholera and tuberculosis were rife and for years no one really knew how they spread. Penny licks were typically returned to the seller and re-filled for the next customer, sometimes without even being washed. Following scientific revelations, penny licks were banned in 1899 – to be replaced with the more hygienic waffle cone.

Today, glass collectors are just as likely to focus on something much more modern.

One company, with a history rooted much earlier than the Georgian period, and which survived for centuries afterwards, is Whitefriars. At the end of the thirteenth century, the company emerged on the site of a former monastery, alongside the Thames in London and within easy reach of necessary raw materials. The glassware was named for the white-clad monks who once lived where the glassmakers worked. And its furnaces stayed alight there until the company moved to new premises in Harrow, Middlesex, in the 1920s, where it was in production until its closure in 1980.

Among *Bargain Hunt* teams, Whitefriars distinctive and multi-coloured bark pattern vases have become favourite items, easily spotted across a crowded antiques fair. One such tangerine vase from the 1960s' range was bought for £85 and yielded a £10 profit when it sold at auction. (Tangerine is deemed the most commonly found in the Whitefriars range, making its price more attainable, with aubergine, meadow green and lilac attracting the highest prices and cinnamon, potentially the lowest.)

Popular designer Geoffrey Baxter is behind some of Whitefriars' most popular designs, including The Banjo, Coffin and the Drunken Bricklayer.

But for *Bargain Hunt* expert Ben Cooper there's another Whitefriars item that holds special resonance. His great grandfather, William Butler, was the designer of a footed bowl that's had enduring popularity for a century. Although he was a Birmingham-based master craftsman, Butler was invited to produce new lines for Whitefriars. It means that while Ben is looking out for winning buys for *Bargain Hunt* teams, he might encounter a gorgeous piece of glassware with a direct family connection.

Such is the esteem in which Whitefriars glass is now held, even a lookalike can make money at auction. One *Bargain Hunt* team spent £15 on just such a vase and watched in amazement as it sold for £42, giving them a £27 profit.

Given the high prices that Whitefriars glass now commands, Ben has two bits of advice for would-be buyers who want to avoid imitations. Firstly, check the colour of the piece carefully. If you can compare any piece that interests you with the palette used in genuine articles, you might easily spot the difference. Secondly, check the pontil mark on the bottom of the bowl or glass. If it's in evidence, then it's not the genuine article as at Whitefriars, all such imperfections were polished away.

His entry-level advice to anyone wanting to start buying and selling glass is simple. 'Buy what you like, what you are drawn to, and buy what you can afford.'

Before taking the next step, he advocates seeking the help of an expert. 'Go to a specialist glass dealer to make your purchases. You might have to pay a bit more, but you will get that back in terms of the education an expert will offer you in the thirty minutes you spend in his or her company.

'A good dealer wants to nurture you as a return customer. They will let you handle items, and they will have plenty of information in catalogues, as well as everything they have already learned. And they won't force anyone to buy.

'Afterwards, you can buy with confidence and the antique itself comes to life.'

Whitefriars is only one of numerous makers of art glass, and presenter Eric Knowles, who is a lecturer and author who specialises in glass made in the century prior to 1940, knows them all. Not everything is as it seems in the world of glass, he points out.

'Bristol blue glass wasn't just made in Bristol,' he says. 'It was made all over the country. Fundamentally, cobalt oxide – used to colour the glass – was imported through Bristol and that's how a myth grew.'

The cobalt was not so much about adding colour but incorporating a trace element to clear lead crystal that reflects all other colours away from itself, only permitting blue to pass through.

Blue was not the only colour used in glassmaking at the time, with green and amber popular choices. Red was made by adding gold to the mix, a recipe used by the Romans that was rediscovered in Europe in the 1600s, says Eric, and that's why ruby glass, as it became known, was so expensive.

And he went on to unravel yet another mystery. 'Mary Gregory was a glassmaker who worked in Boston and became famous for landscapes.

'For some unknown reason, perhaps to appease the Americans, her name became attached to glass with enamelled children's figures on it. Most "Mary Gregory" art glass that you see was made in what was Bohemia, and is now the Czech Republic.'

The word 'cameo' makes most people think of a brooch, but cameo glass was perfected in Stourbridge in the last decades of the nineteenth century, with brothers Thomas and George Woodall both major figures. Their work was described as 'a pinnacle' by Eric.

He's also an admirer of French glass made by Galle, Daum and Legras, and the makers in Scandinavia, including Kosta Boda and Orrefors.

As if to prove his point, a 1980s' vase by Kosta Boda, an enterprise formed in 1742 in Sweden, was bought by one *Bargain Hunt* team for £45, and sold at auction for £80, making a sizeable £35 profit.

Meanwhile, glass made in the 1950s by Fulvio Bianconi and bearing the brand name Salviati are on Eric's list of desirable makers.

'All these are names that command attention,' he said.

For anyone new to the glass collectors' market he has a few tips:

1. Look for a maker's mark. It makes a huge difference, especially with contemporary items. If pieces are good, you have to wonder why they wouldn't be marked.

2. Many items made by named makers are keenly sought after, but that doesn't mean everything is expensive. Look out for something made by the Yorkshire-based company Bagley, for example, which produced household items made from pressed glass after 1912, in popular Art Deco designs.

3. Although Stourbridge and Bristol are big names in glassmaking, there were also major manufacturers in Manchester, Warrington, Gateshead, Sunderland, Scotland and London.

4. Art glass is best displayed under natural light. If it's in a cabinet, choose LED bulbs as you don't want hot bulbs on glass. The glass contains different metallic elements, which will expand and retract at different levels, putting stresses on the internal structure.

5. If you choose to put a piece on a windowsill, beware
   of sunny days when glass can magnify sunrays.
   I scorched my wooden windowsill that way. And
   remember that cold weather can fracture glass,
   so take it off the sill on winter nights.

Waterford Crystal is another anomaly, with a history in two parts. Glassmaking began in the Irish city back in the late eighteenth century, and it gained a fine reputation for cut flint glass. But a toxic blend of industrial troubles, including a range of punitive taxes, ended the venture well before the turn of the twentieth century.

It wasn't until after the Second World War that a Czech refugee Karel Bacik arrived in Ireland to set up a crystal factory. He sought out experienced Czech craftsman, Miroslav Havel, who drew inspiration from original designs stored by the National Museum in Dublin. Thanks to the pair, a new glassmaking tradition was established. Waterford Crystal is typically cut by a diamond-edged wheel to maximise the reflection of light.

Miroslav Havel is not a name on everybody's lips these days but some glass artists went on to become household names. The most famous, of course, is René Lalique. Born in the Champagne region of France in 1860, Lalique made jewellery before turning his attention to glass, and produced elegant figures with a characteristic frosted finish, some early examples of which can sell for thousands of pounds today. At first, he worked in the Art Nouveau style that was popular at the time. But as time and tastes changed, he moved seamlessly into Art Deco. But his passion for glass didn't stop at sculpture, as Roo explains.

'He was a visionary, designing the chandeliers and glass lighting for the first-class dining room on the iconic SS *Normandie*. He designed for the Côte d'Azur Pullman Express, and even for Japanese royalty.

More accessible still, his collaboration with perfume makers Coty from 1907 brought forth a distinctive range of scent bottles. There were car mascots, vases and table ornaments too. He marked his work with a variety of signatures, which may have been stencilled, etched, moulded or engraved and have subsequently been faked many times. It takes considerable experience to make a judgement on a Lalique piece.

After his death in 1945 – when the R disappeared from the official Lalique signature – the company continued in the hands of his children, then his granddaughter. The business was eventually sold in 1997 and even today the brand name continues to loom large.

In broad terms, post-war Lalique is less expensive than anything made before the 1940s, with contemporary pieces selling second-hand for a fraction of their retail cost.

A modern Lalique sparrow bought by one *Bargain Hunt* team alert to the prestigious name, was bought for £50 and sold at auction for £80.

'Lalique is defined by a giddy, intoxicating combination of beauty, quality, effervescence, skill and rarity, which makes this one of the most sought-after names in glass,' says Roo.

Tiffany is another high-end glass marque, associated with decorative lampshades. The brand is named for Louis Comfort Tiffany, an artist who found a passion for stained glass. His father Charles was the founder of the jewellery chain Tiffany & Co, made famous in the 1961 film *Breakfast at Tiffany's*, starring Audrey Hepburn.

As for Louis, he was a successful painter until he became obsessed with the chemistry behind coloured glass, questing for different tones and textures. Thanks to him, a thin, patinated metal was used to join delicate pieces of glass, replacing the thick lead rods that were previously used. The ensuing elegance of the Art Nouveau lampshades was popular in the last quarter of the nineteenth century and first decade of the twentieth.

But public tastes changed and Tiffany shades suffered a catastrophic fall from grace. In the 1930s, Tiffany's work was so unpopular in America that shades were broken up so people could cash in on the metal work that held them together.

At the head of the once-prestigious firm was Accrington-born Joseph Briggs. He'd worked his way up from dogsbody to master craftsman, and finally had the unenviable task of closing down operations in New York. Briggs returned to Accrington with crates of Tiffany products, much of which he donated to the borough. Since the 1970s, the items have been on display at the Haworth Art Gallery, which Eric says is well worth a visit.

Since childhood, Eric, who lived close to Accrington and has been a regular visitor to the museum and, in due course, became a Tiffany expert.

'Tiffany made 500 different shades and almost as many different bronze bases,' he explains. 'Some bases were made specifically to go with a shade while some were interchangeable.

'You can only appreciate a Tiffany lamp when it is illuminated, just as with stained glass in a church, that you can only see when you go inside.'

'Most of us won't purchase a Lalique or Tiffany product, but that doesn't mean you won't get an opportunity to buy some glass art. And the usual rules apply when buying glass for your home; get it because you like it, not for the maker's mark on the bottom.'

One team on the show did just that and bought an iridescent pedestal bowl for £10. It was deemed carnival wear by the auctioneer, the kind of novelty item that might once have been won at a fun fair. Nonetheless, it sold for £18, bringing the team a welcome £8 profit.

Alongside decorative glass, there came the mundane. When glass was mass manufactured from the nineteenth century, its uses proliferated and bottles were used for everything from milk to medicines.

Vintage milk bottles might attract some interest at auction, especially if they bear unusual names or marks, although scent bottles are more numerous at antiques fairs and are usually a better buy. Always check for small chips on the rim and test the stopper before purchase. If it's a snug fit, it is most likely the original.

Best Buy

An oversized perfume bottle, used for shop windows rather than a dressing table, is called a factise and the best examples are collectible. They were often filled with a cheap liquid to impersonate pricey fragrance. One team sniffed out a hefty profit when they found one.

Bought £50 Sold £230 Profit £180

For some people, the heaving tables of antiques fairs aren't the only places to seek antique glass. Collectors who have located Victorian bottle tips get digging and turn up nuggets of social history. As a child, Caroline Hawley used to dig for old bottles and keep her treasures in a box under her bed.

Initially, fizzy drinks were sold in stoneware bottles, not least to disguise their unappetising appearance. But after 1870, Codd bottles were used, distinguished by a marble sealed into position to prevent a loss of gas. When it was time for a drink, the marble was pushed down inside the bottle, into a lug that held it to one side while the liquid gushed out. The bottles took their name from inventor Hiram Codd, a cork salesman determined to perfect the storage of carbonised drinks.

For Caroline, the quest was for an undamaged Codd bottle. 'At the time, kids used to break them to get the marble out,' she explains. 'It was almost impossible to find one that was whole.'

'The small wooden object used to open the bottle was called a Codd's walloper. Hence the expression, "A load of old codswallop!".'

Recently, Caroline's auctioneering company sold a ginger beer bottle for £1,500.

Victorian bottles are also often liberated from ash pits, the sites where collections of household ash were deposited, giving bottles thrown away at the time a soft landing. Vintage bottles do yield impressive prices at auction with one reaching £2,000 at an auction in 2021.

Considerably rarer and more prized still are shaft and globe bottles, which date from the seventeenth century. One such bottle, apparently dug up on a Cornish moor, was sold for £8,300 in 2018. The exceptional price was reached for the onion-shaped bottle even with damage to its rim and neck. However, do remember you need permission to dig up items on land you don't own.

Analyse That: Quality of Craftsmanship

Even with years of experience, John Cameron admits it is easy to overlook the quality of craftsmanship when you are balancing all the other aspects of an item during valuation.

'With experience you will be able to differentiate between fine, good and poor craftsmanship. Usually, if something is handmade and displays a reasonably high standard of workmanship, it is likely to have originally been an expensive purchase, and probably an item aimed at the upper classes. The materials used will usually offer the first clue, but there is no substitute for recognising fine workmanship and attention to detail. In terms of potential value, there is also a difference between "quality" machine-made items and "cheap" mass-produced machine-made items. Since Ancient times, man has made items to suit all budgets and at first glance one can be forgiven for thinking things look the same. But investigate further and quality will always shine through. Look closely at a piece of wooden fretwork, for example, and you should see where the craftsman's saw has been repositioned as it follows the curves and shapes of the design. On pre-machine age furniture, the screws will have been hand-cut so the slots on the head won't all be dead centred. The veneers on furniture too, when cut by hand, will be around 2mm thick, whereas they are micro-thin on machine-made pieces.'

6

SILVER

Strolling around an antiques fair with an expert leaves the *Bargain Hunt* teams in their wake and audiences at home in rapt admiration.

Just a glance at a busy cabinet and the know-how soon shines through. Be they auctioneers or dealers, the experts can identify the purpose of a mysterious object, what it is made of, how it was made and what it might be worth.

Dating antiques is also usually the preserve of the experts, but when it comes to silver, the door is ajar for any enthusiastic amateur.

That's because silver bears a hallmark – a row of emblems, characters or numbers impressed into the soft metal's surface, containing a code that betrays the 'who, where and when' of each piece.

Silver hallmarks date back to medieval times when they acted as an early form of consumer protection. Since then, it's been understood that if an item doesn't carry a hallmark, then it probably isn't silver. Hallmarks were applied at recognised assay offices throughout the country and each had its own sign, for example, Chester was denoted by three wheat sheaves and a sword, while Newcastle upon Tyne was symbolised by three separate turrets.

Today, there are only four assay offices left to pass judgement on the purity of modern silver. Once, the test involved putting scrapings of the silver into chemicals to gauge the reaction. Now, an X-ray fluorescence machine carries out the necessary investigation in just a few seconds.

Typically, a letter is used to signify the year, although there can be anomalies. Then there are the maker's marks, which might relate to workshops or even sponsors, rather than individual craftsmen and women, although sometimes the name of the actual maker is revealed. In addition, there could be a monarch's head stamped into the silver, proving the necessary tax had been paid.

Even the experts resort to reference books when they are checking the provenance of silver items. If you don't want to cart the necessary reference books around an antiques fair, there's a smartphone app you can use instead.

And, like every golden rule, there are exceptions. Silver is always hallmarked unless it comes from outposts in Ireland where, during British rule, the roads used to reach the assay office in Dublin were haunted by highwaymen. Once there, items that were deemed sub-standard were commandeered and melted down. So Irish silversmiths habitually saved themselves the hazardous trip, as well as the risk of losing their products, by marking items with hallmarks of their own. In Cork and Limerick, the words sterling or sometimes dollar appeared, instead of the official crowned harp of Dublin. Silversmiths in Galway, Kilkenny, Kinsale, Youghal and Waterford typically marked their goods with the initials of the maker. These unusual and rare emblems can now add significantly to the value of an item. The Irish silver trade declined in the 1820s when it became more economical to import items from Sheffield and Birmingham.

Silver artefacts bearing other unusual marks are also sought after, like those from Jersey. Scottish silver makers have a lively fan base as well and their wares usually sell for more money than equivalent items from London and Birmingham, as those English marques are ubiquitous.

And it is through hallmarks that the influx of French craftsmen in the seventeenth century is readily recalled. In 1685, after France's Louis XIV deprived Protestants of their religious freedoms, numerous craftspeople, including silver and goldsmiths, came to England, Wales and Scotland, invigorating the country's cultural output. Their influence can be tracked through the hallmarks they put on their handiwork.

Silver has an enduring appeal. Easily engraved, people buy cake slices or napkin rings and quickly transform them into personalised wedding gifts or christening presents.

Silver can also be forged for practical purposes. Traditionally, nurses were presented with silver buckles on completion of their training, with each buckle bearing an individual and intricate design. The gift was popular in Victorian times when nursing was in its infancy. Pioneers Florence Nightingale and Mary Seacole helped to transform the way patients were cared for during and after the Crimean War. Until then, nursing had been viewed as immodest or improper for young, unmarried women. Afterwards, nursing schools, like the Nightingale Training School at St Thomas's Hospital in London, which opened in 1860, became established.

For decades after that, a silver buckle was the ideal fastener for uniform belts or to fasten the capes that were part of the nursing ensemble. Today, silver nursing buckles hold the interest of some collectors and, generally speaking, the more elaborate the detail, the higher the price. However, one team who spent £40 on one came up just wide of the mark, as it sold at auction for only £32.

Silver can likewise be used for fun-sized items with idiosyncratic appeal. For Catherine Southon, the sale of a pair of Victorian silver salts in the form of kangaroos, for a mammoth £18,000, remains a treasured memory.

This highly adaptable precious metal was also used for other articles that were once in daily use, and these now help to illustrate how life has changed in the last two centuries. During their expeditions around antiques fairs, *Bargain Hunt* teams have found silver snuff boxes, compacts, postage stamp cases, a dedicated bowling ball and thimbles, while silver often features on the collars of glass scent bottles and decanters – all objects rarely found in households today.

Mark Stacey turned his team's loss into profit with a solid silver pill box, with a gilded interior, bought for £20 and sold for £52. A chunky ladle with crisp hallmarks revealing it was made in London in 1800 was bought for £101 by another team and sold for £110. A small profit, but a profit nonetheless.

A silver toast rack dated 1848, which would look as good on a breakfast table today as it did in the Victorian era, made £25 profit, after being bought for £125 and sold for £150.

Caroline Hawley added £20 to her team's total with a bonus buy that she termed 'Edwardian frippery'. The £70 solid silver 'table' was small enough to sit in the palm of her hand, with a pie crust frill around the table top and lion's paw feet on its three legs. The auctioneer had a different word for it: exquisite. And its fundamental lack of purpose these days didn't hold back bidding, with the price quickly reaching £90.

Four solid silver napkin rings, also from the Edwardian period and another find by Caroline, were bought for £30 and made £10 profit when the hammer fell, even though they are rarely used on tables today.

A pair of silver salts dating from 1807 looked good enough for one team to pay £120. They were rewarded with a £10 profit after the tableware sold for £130. And in the same show a silver flask, with a Chester hallmark, dating from 1921 and decorated with a branch and flying swallow, sold for a mighty £160. Expert Kate Bliss had spent just £35 on this bonus buy and she joined the team in winning a golden gavel.

Yet hallmarked silver is no guarantee of making money at auction. An Art Deco sterling silver cigarette case, which cost one team £65, was sold for just £42, giving them a £23 loss. In the same sale, competing glass and silver scent bottles battled it out for supremacy. One lot was a pair of glass bottles with a silver cuff around the necks, which made a £10 profit. But the Edwardian bottle with a silver sleeve was saddled with a £40 loss, after being bought for £95 and sold for just £55 – even though it bore the Chester hallmark that so often enhances value. On items like scent bottles, which bear silver on the stopper and around their rims, ensure the hallmarks match so you know you have the original parts. An Edwardian scent bottle bought for £20 by Danny Sebastian as a bonus buy had a hinged lid, so no doubts on that score with this item. Made of chunky hobnail effect glass, it sold for £35.

Check carefully to make sure an item hasn't been repurposed, warns Catherine Southon. A child's pap boat might be transformed into a gravy boat, or a twin-handled tankard into a jug, and the Victorians were particularly keen to adapt Georgian silver. Look for telltale solder marks and check the hallmarks carefully.

One team discovered that the silver cream jug they bought was in fact a christening cup, with a spout and food latterly soldered into place. The flaw was flagged at the auction house, long after money had changed hands. Modifications like this entail another visit to the Assay offices, where new or additional parts can be tested and hallmarked. Without a certificate saying this had happened, any ensuing sale would contravene the Hallmarking Act 1973. So for once an item bought by a Bargain Hunt team didn't go under the hammer and, for the purposes of the programme, was treated as if it had broken even.

SPOONS

Spoons are one area that tends to excite both buyers and sellers. Silver spoons replaced wooden ones at some time in the medieval period and were used as an everyday endorsement of wealth. Owners would carry spoons around like keys, so they were always at hand at mealtimes. (It was, of course, centuries before forks came to the table.) Even in those early years, silver spoons were given as christening gifts. It's still possible to buy silver spoons dating from the Tudor period, when apostle spoons – sets of thirteen with handles featuring figures of the disciples and Jesus himself – were popular and presented to newborns. When it came into usage in the eighteenth century, the phrase 'born with a silver spoon in his mouth' wasn't necessarily used derisively.

Since the Middle Ages, but especially after Georgian times, silver spoons have been made in all shapes and sizes. There are basting spoons, typically with long handles to distance the user from a spitting meat joint, and berry spoons, distinctive for the fruity decoration in the spoon bowl. Berry spoons are generally Georgian spoons upcycled by Victorian craftspeople. Still, a pair of berry spoons with gold leaf inside the decorated spoon bowls were bought by one *Bargain Hunt* team for £65, and sold for £75, helping the team to win a golden gavel.

Mote spoons, with stencilled bowls, are thought to have been used for skimming the surface of tea and coffee, to remove free-floating grouts. Soup ladles are generally large and sauce ladles tend to be ornate, while snuff spoons are very small. Sugar spoons also have delicately pierced bowls with which to dredge sweetener over fruit. Sugar tongs and nips are also popular silver artefacts.

Cheese scoops are long, with trough-shaped bowls, not to be confused with marrow spoons or scoops, usually double-ended and used to tackle long shafts of bone. No longer used, even a fine example of a marrow spoon can struggle when it comes to auction. A team that bought one dating from 1829, made by a reputable silversmith and with crisp hallmarks as well as a coat of arms, found it made just £75 at auction, exactly half what they paid for it.

Runcible spoons look like sugar shovels but have tines on the tip. A more modern term for them is 'spork' and they are intended for use with pickles and chutney. Caddy spoons, used for taking tea leaves from a container, may be compact but they are often ornate and attract the attention of silver buyers. Sadly, not so with the twentieth-century one bought by one *Bargain Hunt* team for £92 in Narberth, Wales. Despite bearing the name of iconic Danish silversmith Georg Jensen, it sold for just £65. Yet at a different auction, a Georg Jensen cream spoon, dating from 1926 and costing £75, sold for £130, producing a not inconsiderable profit of £55. As always, it depends not only on where the auction takes place, but who turns up to bid!

Still, the lengthening list embraces spoons designed for use with eggs, medicine, mustard and salt, as well as the familiar tea and table spoons, so you can see that collectors have plenty of options. Although they probably didn't know it, those lucky enough down the ages to eat off silver spoons were probably keeping themselves healthy, as it helps to kill bacteria.

Mystery Object

The name of this spoon with a half-moon covering across its top gave a valuable clue about its use. Called an etiquette spoon, it was once essential to maintain dining room decorum. Its user would have been a man with a mighty moustache, who would no longer finish the first course with particles of soup marooned in his facial hair. The idea was patented in New York in the 1860s and these days the value of etiquette spoons is enhanced because of their rarity.

Sleek design and a warmth to the touch are partly what make silver spoons a popular choice. One team was delighted to buy a set of six spoons for £48 after Ben Cooper admired the fiddle design – named for the shape of the handle – with each bowl joined separately to the spoon stem. Fiddle design was hugely popular in Britain between 1810 and 1880, although it almost vanished after the First World War. Presenter Charlie Ross called the spoons 'very collectible' and auctioneer Philip Serrell declared the lot was 'a quality item'. However, on this occasion bidders begged to differ and the spoons sold for just £30, making a loss of £18.

Happily, for Chuko Ojiri and his team it was a different story. He bought a boxed set of silver spoons, made in Sheffield in 1924, with ten spoons in total as a bonus buy, for just £15. As the auctioneer observed, the condition of the spoons was so pristine they had likely never been used. The set was sold for £50, bringing a £35 profit – and a winning score to the team.

When the art of plating emerged at the start of the industrial age, there emerged a raft of items that bore the appearance of being solid silver but were created at a much-reduced cost.

'It was easy to be misled by the apparent "hallmarks" on a piece,' warns Roo. 'And this deception was intentional. Many makers emulated silver hallmarks on EPNS (Electroplated nickel silver) items. This was an excellent way for people to still impress their guests if they couldn't afford silver!

'Another cost-effective way to impress guests was to have silver collars on cutlery. Inspect your cutlery carefully. The blade might say Sheffield Plate or EPNS, but the collar (the ring that joins the handle to the utensil) may be hallmarked with silver – a lesser amount of it, but silver nonetheless!'

One such mix-and-match set of knives, made in 1938 with silver handles and stainless-steel blades in the original case, was bought for £24 in Grantham, and held its value, selling at £25 at auction.

Still, a piece of silver is worth any money if you know precisely what you want. Philip Serrell was delighted when he found a silver label with the word 'Worcester' engraved on it, made to go around the neck of a condiment bottle. After all, he lives and works in a county famous for a sauce that's been made there since 1837. 'I knew I would have to pay between £150 and £250 for it. But the price didn't matter to me, as it is something I have always wanted.'

Analyse That: Style and Movement

Fashions ebb and flow and tracking them can help place an object in time, says John Cameron.

'Many of you will be familiar with words like "rococo", "neo-classical" and "gothic" but having a more in-depth knowledge of their origins, visual elements and characteristics, not forgetting the designers and craftsmen associated with each style, will help to date, appraise and value most things. It pays to have a mental and visual understanding of the essential characteristics and practitioners of important styles, so a comprehensive decorative arts dictionary is a must for any serious appraiser.

'Rococo, for example, a frivolously light decorative style emerging on the continent circa 1730s and associated with asymmetry and reoccurring "S" and "C" scrollwork, fell from grace, being replaced by neo-classicism during the latter half of the eighteenth century. The style re-emerged during the 1830s as "Rococo Revival", making items from the original period and the later "revival" period hard to differentiate to the untrained eye. This is where an understanding of materials and construction techniques are also considered in combination in the confirming or elimination process. Date, object, materials, maker, style can all be considered as individual elements but they should also be considered as a coherent whole.'

7

VICTORIANA

For Britons, 1837 would prove a remarkable year. The UK suffered a smallpox epidemic, Euston station opened and mathematician Charles Babbage published a paper about a mechanical computer, which he called an Analytical Engine. Yet it's not for these reasons that the date is memorable, but for the dawning of a new age with the accession of Queen Victoria. At the time, her subjects would have no reason to believe this fresh-faced, fleet-footed young woman would preside over a breathtaking technological charge into modern times.

Until then, the throne had been occupied for seven years by her uncle, King William IV. He was already gravely ill when she celebrated her eighteenth birthday. But at his death shortly afterwards, none of his eight surviving illegitimate children could succeed him and the five he'd had with his wife, Queen Adelaide, died at or soon after birth.

Talking about the Victorian era, it's not the personal triumphs or failings of the monarch that stick in the mind but this gear shift in society and its predilections. Today's tastes have veered away from those of a typical Victorian, yet *Bargain Hunt's* Caroline Hawley is a fan of Victorian paraphernalia, even if it has now fallen out of fashion. One of her favourite antiques fair finds from that reign remains a posy holder. Made in silver, gold or gilded metal, the best examples had a finger ring with which to clasp the artefact. 'Today they are only useful to brides but once women held a posy to put under their nose when they went outside, to mask the smell of the streets,' she explains. Back indoors, some examples had legs that would spring out so the posy could stand on a table, as a decoration.

FIRE SCREENS

For the same women in polite society, fire screens were a must-have, as Caroline reveals. 'It was very unfashionable to have a ruddy face, so ladies with pale skins sat behind fire screens to protect their complexions.'

Pole screens, attached to the fireplace, which could swing out before being placed into the appropriate protective position, were, in fact, a Regency period invention that remained popular among Victorians, Caroline explains.

SMOKING HABITS

One of the enduring habits of Victorian England was smoking and for Caroline, that leads to a variety of items that signify the era. She has special affection for the smoker's cap.

'Years ago, when I had a shop, I used to sell these all day long as collectibles. These are velvet, round, tasselled caps with embroidery, worn by gentlemen to protect their hair from the smell of smoke. The same men might also wear smoking jackets and embroidered or beaded slippers.'

Smoking was as much a ritual as a pastime and involved numerous accoutrements. As the British Empire extended its reach, cheroots from India became a must-have and cheroot holders and cases, desirable accessories. A cheroot is like a small cigar and could take between thirty minutes and two hours to smoke. Cases were made in silver, or silver-mounted leather or crocodile skin, probably to accommodate between three and five cheroots. Meanwhile, cheroot holders – particularly important because the smoker needed all the help he could get in not inhaling the noxious fumes – were often made from precious materials and bound with silver. Just as cheroots displaced snuff in polite society, they would themselves be nudged aside by cigarettes.

One *Bargain Hunt* team found a cheroot holder at a modest £16. But the cylinder wasn't made of amber, as they'd hoped it was, and the ring at its end wasn't real silver. One redeeming feature was that it came with a case. However, when it got to auction it made just £15, leaving them with a small loss.

VESTA CASES

When it came to lighting up, well, that wasn't as easy as it might sound. Many tried and failed to finesse the humble match. Initially, it was thought a splint tipped with white phosphorous that ignited with friction was the answer to a prayer for portable, fast flames. But early matches were so hazardously volatile they could fire up even before friction was applied and they were also toxic. One early solution was to secure the matches in a box that had a handy striking surface. One of the early matches was called a vesta, after the Roman goddess of fire and hearth, and the boxes made to house them became known as vesta cases.

Thus, the advent of the vesta box as the Victorian age got underway helped to keep people safe. But boxes also became a must-have novelty item as people needed many to light lamps, domestic fires and for smoking cigarettes, cigars and pipes. A mighty range of styles exists, although most have a flip-top lid, with a ribbed striking area on the base and, often, a link to attach it to a watch chain. Inside, there might well have been a lining to shield the case from match damage. Many were made out of silver that was engraved or chased with motifs, although they were also made in brass at a lesser cost. The most expensive had jewels set into their surfaces, the least pricey bore advertising slogans and the naughtiest depicted semi-clad women in alluring poses. Larger models were produced for table tops.

For collectors of small, neat silver items, a vesta case is an almost obligatory buy. If the decoration or advertising slogan features a locomotive, then it might also bring interest from railway enthusiasts, while those with a painted enamel panel featuring a golfing scene will get a second glance from anyone who plays the sport.

Vesta cases were still popular in the Edwardian era, although by now matches could finally be transported safely in boxes, as harmless red phosphorous was being used, instead of white.

One *Bargain Hunt* edition saw both red and blue teams vying for profits by buying vesta boxes. On this occasion each case dated from the Edwardian era, bore a

Birmingham hallmark and cost £20. Yet when it came to the auction, one doubled its money while the rival merely broke even. The likely cause was a monogram on the side of the unprofitable one, something that tends to always restrict resale value. Given that they were once commonplace and well used, some dinks in the metal are to be expected. But with vesta cases and other small, lidded objects, it is the robustness of the hinge that counts.

Later, *Bargain Hunt* expert Chuko Ojiri thought that the diminutive 1849 vesta box he found as his bonus buy was worth every penny of the £140 he spent. He was so thrilled with the find he called it a work of art. The key was the hallmark that revealed the maker: Nathaniel Mills. In the nineteenth century, Mills and his sons, based in Caroline Street, Birmingham, won a reputation for excellence. The auctioneer, Richard Winterton, conceded it was one of the best names in the business and that it was a rare opportunity to purchase an item made by Nathaniel Mills. However, he drew attention to its battered condition and felt its pattern was uncharacteristically plain. Ultimately, it sold for just £90, leaving a £50 loss for the team.

CALLING CARDS

From today's vantage point, it seems that the average Victorian would have been clattering with cases as he moved around his neighbourhood. In his jacket pocket, alongside his cheroot and vesta cases, he would also have carried another one for calling cards, something considered essential to the well-bred gentlemen of the Victorian period. The habit of leaving a calling card had its roots in Regency England. The etiquette around it was rigid, with size, font and purpose clearly defined and understood, like a code.

The form of calling card cases was limitless, and they might be made of leather, silver, ivory, sandalwood, porcelain, tortoiseshell or mother of pearl. Beyond the construction of the hinged case, the finishing might include laquer, embroidery, engraving or gilding. Silver calling card cases featuring familiar British landmarks, called castle tops, are probably the most desirable, with one made by Nathaniel Mills in 1845 and featuring the Bevis Marks Synagogue in London selling in 2005 for £8,000.

MEN AND WOMEN OF LETTERS

The use of calling cards eventually diminished, although communication was improving in leaps and bounds. A key innovation from the Victorian era was the modern postal network, which replaced a haphazard system with its roots in privilege and wealth. Thanks to the introduction of an inexpensive stamp – the Penny

Black – writing and receiving letters was open to all. Sir Rowland Hill was the man behind the plan, initiating one uniform cost, regardless of distance and pre-paid by the sender. The appearance of adhesive stamps in 1840 only accelerated the changes.

Before Hill's time, senders had to take their mail to village inns or turnpikes for collection by coaches. Post boxes in different shapes and sizes were now installed around the country for easy dispatch, and even today it's possible to gauge the Victorian history of a street or area by the presence of a box with the initials VR on the front. Initially, most were green in colour and they weren't painted red until 1874. It wasn't until the twentieth century that pillar boxes were made as free-standing, smooth-sided cylinders. Smaller post boxes, attached to posts and bearing the ciphers of George V and VI, have recently become a target for thieves, looking to sell them to antiques buyers.

Today, a Penny Black, bearing the profile of Queen Victoria, is of interest to stamp collectors, but is not especially rare as so many were made. As always, condition is key and one in excellent condition might sell for several hundred pounds today. For collectors, every single stamp is a miniature masterpiece, but some have assumed extraordinary value today. Although a contemporary of the Penny Black, the Two Penny Blue is far rarer and those issued in Mauritius in 1847, at the time a British colony, are especially so. One surviving stamp became the most expensive ever sold in Britain when it was auctioned for £1 million in 2011.

Hill's ideas caused political controversy at the time, although the most startling result of the new procedure was a dramatic increase in the volume of paid postage.

As a result of Hill's vision, letter writing became an established literary form. That led to a boom in pens, to deliver ink onto the page. Quill pens were replaced by fountain pens, which in turn made way for ballpoint pens after they were invented in the 1880s. Still, there's a niche market today for fountain pens, with Mont Blanc and Conway Stewart being names to notice, and gold nibs among the more unusual finishes.

Other writing implements also had their place and one £40 bonus buy from John Cameron was a 9-carat gold mechanical pencil, with a bloodstone seal on its top, still in its original box and bearing the name of its maker in Bridport, Dorset. At auction, it doubled its money.

Alongside the inkwell, you might also have found a pounce pot on Victorian desks. Looking very much like pepper pots, they contained crushed pumice stone, cuttlefish shell or even talcum powder. The writer would first scatter the pounce powder over paper to absorb grease marks, then use it at the end of the letter-writing process to dry excess ink. One Bargain Hunter bought a hallmarked silver pounce pot for £55. This one was made after the Victorian era and the auctioneer suspected, by the shape of the dome, it was in fact a pepperette. Perhaps those two reasons combined to bring about an auction price of £50, and a £5 loss to the team.

The days of the fountain pen, mechanical pencil and pounce pot were numbered as technology marched on with the advent of the typewriter. Their use became widespread from the 1880s and they dominated for a century, until the advent of computers. A *Bargain Hunt* team thought they might write a bit of history when they bought a later Imperial typewriter for £49. The original Imperial machine was designed by American-Spanish immigrant Hidalgo Moya, who went into business in Leicester in 1908. A vast range of models was bought out over the years, and each can be dated through a serial number. But, as expert Caroline Hawley pointed out, so many typewriters were made in that one-hundred-year spell that there's still no shortage of them today. And, unless they are going to be decorative, only populations without a regular electricity supply have use for them now. The hammer went down on the typewriter at just £12.

POSTCARDS

Plain postcards became available in 1870 and some twenty-five years later, picture postcards went on sale.

Images of people and places were widely available and collecting postcards became something of a craze in the early years of the twentieth century, prior to the First World War. Today, they offer a glimpse into fashions and the geography of years ago, with stunning vistas and farm animals also getting in the picture.

Mystery Object

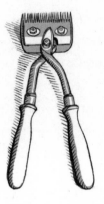

It's not a back scratcher or a hearth scrape. This stumpy tool with a hollow brass handle, a valve and a wide, toothy end was used for grooming horses in Victorian and Edwardian times. The handle was filled with paraffin, which was burned via a wick. Stray hairs on the horses were then singed off, with horses apparently enjoying the heat while it was done. Electric clippers are now the preferred option.

Another change that transformed British life was the arrival of an organised police force for the nation. Politician Sir Robert Peel had launched a police force in London as early as 1829, called Bobbies or Peelers, who were widely distrusted as an instrument of government suppression. A decade later, and counties across the country were permitted to form a police force, although it wasn't until the 1850s that they became mandatory. The earliest policemen wore top hats and were armed only with truncheons, a weapon inherited from the constables and watchmen employed in towns and parishes since the Middle Ages to keep the peace. In Victorian times, truncheons carried a royal crest or a constabulary coat of arms, with markings to indicate rank. There's a growing market for truncheons, as one *Bargain Hunt* team discovered, spending £40 on one at an antiques fair and selling it at auction for £70.

Being an Auctioneer

Every auction is a piece of improvised theatre, with the rostrum its stage. It's salesmanship, certainly, but, when it's done well, it has the gusto and flourish of a Shakespearean drama. What fuels the auctioneer is a love of the objects going under the hammer. Without that, explains Nick Hall, it could be any commodity being sold. 'You have to have the passion, to see what the collectors are seeing.'

From his or her vantage point, the auctioneer must 'read the room', which means identifying at least two people who might push up the price. Beyond that, it's a case of monitoring a cascade of internet and telephone bids that may well come in at the same time. Recognising the bids as they are being made – a raised eyebrow or an almost imperceptible nod – is no mean feat, but auctioneers can always discern buyers from bystanders. The aim is to get good value for a vendor, although there are no guarantees. It's also the auctioneer's job to keep the mood buoyant, even when the bids grind to a halt.

1. 'It's like being a conductor of an orchestra,' explains Catherine Southon. 'There are bids in the room, on the internet, on the telephone and those made in advance. It's a case of making everything work together and in harmony.'

2. 'You've got to know what you don't know as well as recognising something that's valuable,' says JP. Once a gap in knowledge has been identified, a bit more research can add a lot more interest.

3. 'Auctioneers must have complete authority and be absolutely in charge during proceedings,' declares Kate Bliss, among the first female auctioneers to take to the rostrum.

4. As a young man, Raj Bisram decided he wanted to work in an auction house. 'I wrote to everyone and they all turned me down. The only thing I could do was start my own business.' That was some thirty years ago and since then, Raj has been a regular on the rostrum. 'As an auctioneer, you are putting on a show. You have to make it as entertaining as you possibly can.'

5. Charlie Ross agrees, saying, 'It's not unlike being in a play or musical; the main difference is that you don't have to learn any words – you just decide your own narrative as the auction unfolds.'

6. Once an auctioneer at Bonhams, Eric Knowles hit on an unorthodox style. 'I used to make people laugh. It is much easier to take money off people if they are laughing,' he observed.

7. Presenter Natasha Raskin Sharp had a short, sharp lesson in auctioneering style, thanks to her mum.

'I'd been working in an auction house for only six months when I asked if I could try auctioneering,' she explains.

'My mum stood right in front of the rostrum and filmed the whole thing. I genuinely thought that it went brilliantly and when the auction was over everyone was very polite and told me just how well I had done. Later that day, when I watched the video, I swiftly realised that I had, in fact, been absolutely *dire* – I was like a rabbit caught in headlights! Thank goodness my mum was there and thank goodness the auction house was willing to give me another go.'

8

FURNITURE

When it comes to furniture, dealers are hoping brown will be the new white. Thirty years ago, brown furniture, made from woods like mahogany and walnut, commanded big money in auction houses up and down the country.

However, when fashions changed, prices plummeted. One *Bargain Hunt* team had such faith in the appeal of two oak chairs dated by the auctioneer to the reign of William of Orange that they paid £180. When it came to the auction, they sold for just £10. A bargain considering their age and fine craftsmanship.

For several decades, customers have been favouring pale, flat-packed items despite the chore of having to make them themselves. And if it's not brand-new items in demand, it's furniture from the sixties and seventies. More of that, later.

'The dip in value of brown furniture started in the eighties,' explains *Bargain Hunt* presenter Charlie Ross. 'People started living in a more minimalist style, in houses or flats with smaller room sizes. And, in all honesty, furniture had got overpriced, with quite ordinary things making a lot of money.

'One advantage now is that you can now buy well-made furniture quite cheaply.'

Although there's evidence of furniture in ancient civilisations, it wasn't a great feature of daily life. In the Middle Ages, furniture was scarce and evidence of it remains rare. So, for British Bargain Hunters, the history of furniture – fixed with pegs or nails – begins with the age of oak, which began in about 1500 and lasted for at least a century. Wealthy homes had throne-style chairs, hall cupboards and four-poster beds. Poorer families had settles for seating and kept their belongings in oak chests. It's also known as vernacular furniture.

From 1600, oak gave way to walnut, at about the same time furniture-makers were making significant technical strides. Planks were being cut thinner than before and the art of fitted drawers improved. Once again, the rich had the best items on show, with walnut's characteristic mirrored patterns popular on bureaus and tables. As well, an influx of workers from France – refugee Huguenots escaping religious persecution – helped to introduce more elegant styles. However, cold winters at the beginning of the eighteenth century killed off

Europe's walnut trees and the sun set on the age of walnut furniture when France banned exports in 1720.

At about the same time, British cabinet-makers were gaining access to woods from the New World thanks to burgeoning trade routes, and mahogany, maple and cherry were now the staples. With harder, straighter grains came simpler, more elegant designs. Mahogany proliferated after the scrapping of import taxes in 1733, at the same time as the techniques of craftsmen in the industry were forging ahead, and the age of English country house furniture dawned.

Apart from wood, the other primary influence on British furniture was Thomas Chippendale, the Yorkshire-born designer who set his principles of construction down in the widely circulated pattern book, *The Gentleman and the Cabinet Maker's Director* in 1754. In it were 161 engraved plates, illustrating what Chippendale titled 'Elegant and useful design of household furniture in Gothic, Chinese and Modern Taste'

Of course, Thomas himself wasn't responsible for sawing and sanding every item that today bears his name. The word Chippendale is a by-word for furniture produced in his workshops or to the exacting principles laid down in his book. Chippendale furniture remains highly valued today.

One unfortunate valuer in the trade recently described a pair of green-and-white painted armchairs as French, possibly twentieth century, before giving them a value of up to £150. Fortunately, the internet spared everyone's blushes after some cannier dealers realised they were in fact signature models from the Chippendale workshop in the 1770s and, as a consequence, bidding went up to £50,000. 'This is what we in the trade call "a sleeper",' JP explains.

Also, have some pity for the poor auctioneer, who might be faced with difficult-to-spot forgeries, says JP.

'A dozen Georgian chairs are exponentially more valuable than a set of six,' he explains. 'One way of multiplying the value of a smaller set was to take them to a workshop and take them apart, before matching the original pieces with reproduction ones. Each chair might have two legs that are original, plus a back or seat. A skilled forger can make the task of spotting a fake extremely hard.'

From 1800, decoration became richer in design and more imaginative, with curvy cabriole legs rather than straight ones, perhaps ending in a ball and claw carving.

One example of how craftsmanship with wood advanced was the popular Davenport desk. This compact item, with one area designated for writing and the rest filled with discreet drawers and secret shelves,

was originally commissioned by a Captain Josiah
Davenport from Gillows of Lancaster in the Regency
era and he needed it for a ship, most likely a
merchantman rather than a Royal Navy vessel. As time
unfolded, the Davenport desk became ever more
elaborate in design, with decorative inlays and carvings.
The most surprising looked like a piano until the top
was lifted to reveal pen trays, inkwells, pigeonholes and
more. 'These were very popular in the Victorian period,'
notes Caroline Hawley, and she's still an advocate for
these diminutive triumphs of organisation today, when
living space is often at a premium.

A child's chair was something of a feature of Victorian
times too, and Caroline had several when her own
children were growing up. Small but sometimes ornate,
chairs like these were often used to display collections
of dolls or teddy bears. Today, there's little appetite
for them.

'Times have changed,' she acknowledges. 'Houses tend to be minimalist now and there are not as many doll and teddy collectors as there were. Children's chairs aren't useful, long-term items.'

Victorian furniture tends to reflect a melting pot of styles and influences. Walnut made a reappearance, with slivers of machine-cut veneer making it an option for craftsmen again after an absence of a century or so. One item of Victorian furniture that's largely sunk from view is the loo table, with a round or circular top likely covered by walnut veneer. It was made for the card game Lanterloo, also known as loo, and had a mechanism that allowed the playing surface to be tipped upright, for easy storage. Lanterloo – a game of trumps – had been popular since the seventeenth century, but its star dimmed in Victorian times, although loo tables were still used for breakfast or in halls. A *Bargain Hunt* team purchased a loo table for £75, and it sold at auction for £100, giving them a 33 per cent profit margin.

There are a number of made-to-last Victorian objects that do warrant a place in today's homes, including bow-front chests of drawers and large wardrobes because both hold plenty of clothing and cost very little. And thanks to its practical application, Caroline believes a passion for old-style furniture is finally catching on again.

'I'm excited to see a few young people buying pieces of brown furniture,' she says. 'It is so much cheaper than having furniture built-in or flat-packed, and, if they change their minds, they can sell it again.'

Alongside higher-end furniture, the humble pine wooden box has remained popular. These have long been a feature of furniture history, with the earliest examples dug out from one solid piece of timber. Indoors, flat-topped chests could be used for storage and seating. Domed-topped examples were chosen to repel the rain. It was in Elizabethan times that chests became adorned with intricate carving and might now include drawers, making the basic six-planked box suitable for castles as well as more humble homes. Later still, chests were used as trunks as early emigrants moved around the British Empire and across America.

The popularity of the pine chest is apparent in today's antiques market. One *Bargain Hunt* team espied an example at an antiques fair and were not deterred, despite its well-worn appearance. The box was bought for £15, with expert Caroline Hawley pointing out the presence of a section for candles built into the side because they deterred insect infestations. It sold at £45, three times the amount the team paid for it.

Usually, furniture commands a higher price when it is compact and useful. However, rules are made to be broken and there's a substantial grey area today, as *Bargain Hunt* buyers have revealed.

A whatnot, a set of shelves made to hold decorative items, which usually has carved spindles, isn't necessarily on the top of the shopping list for new homeowners. Yet a Regency-style example, made from mahogany, made one Bargain Hunter a £15 profit, after it was bought for £40 and sold for £55.

Rarely used in the era of central heating, a hand-carved fender stool from the eighteenth century, used for propping feet in front of a fire or by children as a seat, cost just £45. Its virtues, of being well made and decorative, won out at auction where it sold for £95, giving a substantial £50 profit.

And despite the need for small furniture in most houses today, an elm bench was sold for three times its purchase price of £35.

There may yet be no coming back for stand-alone wardrobes, with so many being built into bedrooms these days, but other wooden furniture can be ebonised to make it black or painted in a variety of colours or effects, making it more appealing to modern buyers.

To furnish a house with pieces made years ago is a perfect way to sidestep today's harmful throwaway economy, says JP.

'If a sofa has a sturdy frame, then it will last for generations,' he points out. 'Look underneath at the frame. Hopefully it is oak. You will see all the staple marks in the wood, revealing just how many times it has been refurbished before. This will give an indication of its age. When it is recovered, it will be as good as new.'

Mouse in the House

It's notoriously difficult to determine or distinguish the work of famous furniture-makers as traditionally, few put labels or stamps on their work. It's down to a discerning eye and a reference-book mind to trace styles and hallmarks to reveal who created it. However, some pieces of collectible furniture are easier to identify than others. If you see a sturdy oak seat or table with a carved mouse on a leg, then you've spotted some Mouseman furniture. The man behind it was Yorkshire-born Robert Thompson who, aged eighteen, began working in his father's joinery. His passion became gothic oak furniture and, after working in Ampleforth Abbey, hit upon the trademark for which he became best known. Most of his furniture that's sought today was made in the 1930s, with peg construction, iron fittings and leather coverings.

When it comes to furniture, it's difficult to take the temperature of bidders at auction. One nest of tables dating from the Arts and Crafts period bought for £30 turned a £15 profit at auction, when auctioneer Raj Bisram had backed them to double their money. At another venue, a G-Plan nest of tables made from teak was bought for £45 and sold for £70.

Indeed, nowadays a 1970's sideboard might well fetch considerably more money than a Georgian bureau. Even early IKEA pieces are exciting interest among collectors, with the 'Cavelli' beech-and-fabric chair designed in 1958 by Scandinavian designer Bengt Ruda made prior to the era of flat-pack, selling for more than £12,000 in a Swedish sale.

Prices on furniture made between the 1950s and 1970s are now increasing, says Stephanie Connell, as people look with a different eye on tables, chairs and cabinets made within living memory.

Danny Sebastian puts it more strongly. 'Mid-twentieth-century furniture is the next antique in line after Art Deco – and it is on fire.

'Older generations used to understand and appreciate antique furniture but their numbers are dwindling. Now a younger generation understands that their parents or their grandparents had this more modern furniture. It was around them when they were growing up. They understand it and they like it. People were pushing boundaries back then, it was a funky period.'

At the time, people were responding to the Utility furniture that had been one of the hallmarks of the Second World War in homes everywhere. It was made with the shortages of timber in mind and reflected the mores of the Arts and Crafts movement. After the conflict ended, there was a desire for something different.

It's not the end for traditional antique furniture though, Danny says. 'Top of the tree will always sell. But gone are the days when antiques have to be one hundred years old. That is the old rule of thumb. Now it is the broad umbrella of decorative arts that matters more.'

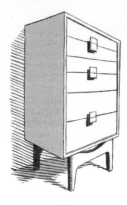

For him, G Plan stands out as a prime example of furniture from the Mid-twentieth century era. (The 'G' stands for Gomme, the former name of the furniture manufacturer that had been in business for decades before hitting the height of fashion.) It comes in two distinct phases: firstly, when it was an entirely British enterprise and later, in the early sixties, when a Danish designer was brought in. There's a tendency for sellers to label everything G Plan as part of its Danish range. Work by the designer in question, Ib Kofod-Larsen, is relatively rare and should bear a gold stamp that includes his signature. Earlier items are more likely to bear a gold-embossed stamp dominated by the letters EG, with the place name of High Wycombe running around its outside. From 1965, labels replaced the stamps, coming in red and white and red and gold, with different styles and fonts applying to set dates. But beware, as labels can be peeled off and reapplied to furniture in the way that stamps can't.

After the war, ercol became known for making Windsor chairs and its use of elm, previously shunned by furniture-makers for its capacity to fracture. The company was started more than a century ago by Lucian Ercolani, who had moved to London's East End from his native Italy when he was a boy. He left school early, but went back to education after seeing a poster for Shoreditch Technical Institute, advertising a course in furniture design. The company, which has been handed down through the generations, is famous for its chic design classics. One *Bargain Hunt* team found a set of four ercol chairs with an unusually ornate back. Their expert, Danny Sebastian, pointed out that these seats were dark in colour when blond is considered the most desirable ercol tint and presenter Natasha Raskin Sharp conceded that, at first glance, they did not look like conventional ercol designs at all. Still, the seats sold for £50, yielding a £6 profit.

Parker Knoll, famous for its sprung chairs, was created after collaboration by a longstanding British furniture maker and a First World War pilot, who pioneered sprung seating after suffering discomfort in the cockpit of his aircraft. Then there are other, more elevated, brands to look out for, including Charles and Ray Eames, Nathan, Archie Shine and Joe Colombo. A wing-backed chair designed by Denmark's Arne Jacobsen became famous for its use in a James Bond film, by the villain Blofeld. Expert Colin Young bought just such a chair as a bonus buy for his team, for £113. Their faith in him was rewarded when it sold for £170.

Typically, the most popular pieces of mid-century furniture were made from teak or rosewood. The accepted wisdom at the moment is that sixties' furniture is highly desirable and that gavels are coming down on record prices. But again, guidelines can go out of the window when it comes to bargain hunting, and here are some examples of how.

A Nathan cabinet championed by Danny Sebastian was bought for £50 by one *Bargain Hunt* team but made a £10 loss at auction.

One team decided a well-made Danish tiled coffee table was exactly what they'd like in their own homes. It was sixty years old, and furniture from that era is generally selling well. However, it was bought for £85 but only made £50 at auction.

Danny also believes that upcycling and recycling old furniture chimes well with younger people today. Still, not every upcycling story has a happy ending, as he discovered when his *Bargain Hunt* team, with seconds to go, opted for a seventies' sideboard featuring a recently added angular white chalk paint design. The make was Castle, not one of the desirable brands, he told his teams. Still, they paid £75 to secure their big buy. When it came to selling the item, however, the first bid the auctioneer could muster was for just £1. It finally sold for £15, leaving them with a painful £60 loss.

And don't take furniture at face value. As one *Bargain Hunt* team discovered, an item may not be all it seems. The pair were delighted to buy a children's rocking chair at Grantham for £80, imagining it had a fine history in a country home. In fact, it was a converted nursing chair, hence the shortened legs. Evidence of the pink draylon covers and live woodworm seemed to pass them by at the time of purchase, but auction attendees were more alive to the drawbacks. It finally sold for £35.

If you think that brown is back in town but are wary about the possible pitfalls, Roo has some tips when it comes to furniture shopping:

1. The wood used can pinpoint the era. Also, look out for expensive wood being used at the front of an item, masking cheaper varieties hidden in the construction.

2. Patina is crucial and beautiful antique chairs will have worn patches on an armrest, for example, where the wood or leather has worn away.

3. Antique furniture will have that musty attic smell, which, although it may not be too pleasant, is the smell of hundreds of years of living memories.

4. Look at the materials, to ensure they aren't modern. And check up on visible signs of craftsmanship, like reinforced joints.

If you still need persuading that brown furniture should be making a comeback, there's one figure that might help you make up your mind. The carbon footprint of a Georgian chest of drawers, already with age and craftmanship on its side, has a carbon footprint that amounts to one-fifteenth of its new flat-pack alternative.

Analyse That: Supply and Demand

Anything that's on trend is likely to command top dollar, explains John Cameron, while objects at the other end of that scale will be far less expensive.

'The price an item will make at auction is driven by demand, and demand is usually influenced by fashion. For example, during the 1970s many people were covering the period panelled doors and spindle-turned staircase balustrades in their Victorian houses with hardboard sheets painted in plain colours.

'Fireplaces and plaster ceiling roses were mercilessly torn from the homes they had occupied since the turn of the last century and thrown into skips. During the mid-1980s, the pendulum of taste swung back towards a more traditional look. People started removing the hardboard panelling and stripping the thick layers of paint from wooden surfaces throughout the home. Reclamation yards satisfied the growing demand for reinstalling Victorian cast-iron fireplaces, butler sinks, baths and other period features. Victoriana was "in" and rising prices in shops and auction houses reflected the growing demand for the "antique look".

'As the supply of genuine Victorian fireplaces and baths was finite, supply could not be increased, except with modern reproductions, therefore prices for original pieces rose. The economic theory of supply and demand can be applied to ALL areas of the fine and decorative arts.'

9

KITCHEN AND GARDEN

kitchen is at the heart of every household. It's the room where domestic life unfolds from breakfast, through coffee time to dinner and late-night snacks. Stew-makers and cake bakers gather there to help the resident family survive and thrive. Lucky cooks use fine implements handed down to them by parents or grandparents, while the rest of us may choose to bring something vintage from the auction room to add to the array of necessary kit, so as to enhance a kitchen's character.

COPPER PANS

From Renaissance times, copper pans have been the indicator of a superior kitchen. Except for silver, copper has the highest conductivity of metals, meaning it heats up and cools down faster than any other metals. It's also known for having antimicrobial properties, so it's a bacteria killer. However, as popular as they have been through modern history, there are some downsides.

Copper doesn't react well with acids, so pans have traditionally been tin-lined. When the lining wears out, they need to be relined, and these days the tin inner is sometimes replaced with stainless steel. The challenge of tin linings has been in evidence for many years.

According to a 1913 manual, *The Principles of Practical Cookery* by E E Mann, its quality is paramount.

'If allowed to become very hot by a flame up the side, while the pan is only partly filled with liquid, the tin is likely to melt; a poor quality is certain to do so.' Once the tin has melted and run down the sides of the pan, the residue forms 'roughnesses that are difficult if not impossible to clean perfectly'.

Enamel-lined iron pans are fine while new, the writer admits, but warns: 'the lining soon becomes covered with little cracks and eventually chips off.'

Then there's the elbow grease needed for copper products to keep them gleaming. The same goes for two popular copper alloys: brass, a mix of copper and zinc, and bronze, which is copper blended with tin.

The 110-year-old manual delivers dire warnings about the need for cleanliness regarding pans.

'Brass, copper, steel and tin are all used for pans, and where well kept – clean and dry – are all good; but otherwise the two first become dangerously unwholesome; and the two last are soon worn through by the action of rust.'

If the kitchens of stately homes and London townhouses glistened with shiny copper pans and sparkling brass or bronze devices, it was because there was an army of servants to do the hard graft necessary to keep them that way. Among the cleaning agents recommended in the book, published just before the nation's social order radically pivoted with the First World War, are soda, Brook's soap, Sapolio, sand, whiting, or pulverised chalk, Pickering's Paste – made from rottenstone – Bath brick, blacklead and emery powder or paper.

Still, there remains an appetite for some copper, bronze and brass kitchenware, as Bargain Hunters have discovered. A sturdy copper cauldron, its handle and clasps in robust condition despite some considerable age, was bought for £55, but auctioned for £60.

An Art Deco plate-copper-and-brass plate warmer, dating from the turn of the twentieth century, was bought by one *Bargain Hunt* team for £100. Their expert JP advised them it was a sound buy after spotting the stamped name on it, W A S Benson. Designer William Arthur Smith Benson, who worked alongside William Morris, was one of the cutting-edge creators of his time. It was, acknowledged the auctioneer, a quality item and it sold for £140, yielding a £40 profit.

Best Buy

Eagle-eyed Richard Madley lifted the lid on a sizeable profit when he snapped up a nineteenth-century bronze tureen bonus buy with a clutch of tenners. With bidding starting at £220, it was clear the item would be hot stuff.

Bought £30 Sold £460 Profit £430

One team found a five-piece set of copper and brass utensils that, being both attractive and useful, ticked two boxes that would resonate with purchasers. Bought for a price of £12, it sold for £25, thus doubling the team's money. Its appeal stood the test of time, but would the buyers of a decorative cruet set have the same good fortune?

CRUET SETS

Once, every well-to-do table would be graced with a condiment set to hold salt, vinegar, mustard and the like.

Popular from Victorian times, they were made in glass, silver, ceramics or even Bakelite, and those that date from Georgian and Art Deco periods are particularly collectible, as are some novelty sets.

This one was a fine example, with six crystal bottles in a plated silver holder. But expert Colin Young spotted a problem; the pattern cut into the bottles wasn't uniform, implying previously broken ones had been replaced at some stage. Mismatched items like this, corralled in a set, do affect the price and the team were able to buy this bit of household history for £13.

The auctioneer was doubtful, warning presenter Natasha Raskin Sharp that these items were old-school nowadays. While once it would have attracted an estimate of between £60 and £90, the cruet would most likely sell for under £40. And his view was accurate, with £35 being paid. However, thanks to the bargaining power of the team, they still came away with a healthy profit.

Mystery Object

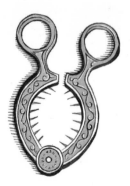

A hinged bracelet with teeth on the inside looks like something from a torture chamber.

Thankfully, its purpose is far more mundane, to take the top off a boiled egg. Undeniably, it makes a neat job, with minimum shell fracture. Still, an unlikely 'must have' when the cost for those made in silver can run into hundreds of pounds.

As Stephanie Connell reminds us, anything being produced in a particular period was the ultimate in technology, fashion and luxury for the time. It's why vintage items offer us a glimpse into another age. But as the decades roll by, the items that were once held so dear by homemakers are left in the wake of new inventions or easier options.

Hence, carved paddles used to shape butter once would have been an aspirational buy for anyone in the rural economy. However, a *Bargain Hunt* team that risked £35 on a pair made a £5 loss at auction, as today they have little use.

Consider laundry day before the arrival of the washing machine. The washing was done in a large bucket, made of wood before metals became commonplace. A laundry dolly – a pronged stick – was used to agitate the clothes. Then the wet washing was wrung out between the rollers of a hand-turned mangle, reducing the drying time by some margin but still, an arduous ritual. Those days have been largely forgotten, although one *Bargain Hunt* team was reminded of the heroics of the weekly wash when they saw a cast-iron mangle. And £95 didn't seem too much to pay for this piece of domestic history. However, at the auction it sold for just £46, probably because it was big and difficult to move. Universally, buyers prefer more easily manoeuvrable objects.

Worst Buy

One blue team tried to recapture their lost childhoods by buying an old, branded ice-cream freezer. No matter that it was eaten by rust and the lid no longer fitted, for them it was worth every penny – even if it could only be used for decorative purposes. Although she's the first to concede that you never know in advance what an item will make, auctioneer Catherine Southon predicted this one would receive a chilly reception and refused to give it floor space at the auction room. 'It's appalling,' she confided before she took to the rostrum, believing it would sell for no more than £10. In the end, not a single offer was made.

Bought £60 No Sale

Many kitchen items from the past decades fall under the bracket of treen, a generic name for small, handmade functional household items.

Once this meant wooden plates and spoons. Today, it's likely to incorporate chopping boards and small bowls. Treen harks back to a time when wood was the accessible material of choice, before the age of cheap metal and glass. More recently still, plastic has usurped treen from the kitchen. In its day, treen was a showcase for carving and turning skills. Of course, time has taken its toll and the number of items is diminishing.

In terms of longevity, stainless steel, a relative newcomer to kitchen cabinets, is faring better. It wasn't until 1914 that the first stainless-steel cutlery was produced. Harry Brearley, of Sheffield, created what he called 'rustless steel' after putting chromium into the metallic mix. His aim was mostly to improve British armaments, but his product soon went on to have many uses. By 1935, stainless steel was used for aircraft, trains, brewing – and kitchen sinks.

In gardens, it's not the metal of choice, being too shiny in a place where a bit of shabby chic goes a long way. One of Gary Pe's teams chose a rusty, green toolbox, which he thought had a military bearing, for £28. The patina was perfect for one auction buyer, who spent £50 to secure it.

Mystery Object

A long cane with a metal spear at one end and a peephole at the other remains a mystery until it becomes clear one works in concert with the other. The peephole is a trigger and, once it's pulled back, the spear opens to reveal serrated edges, perfect for trimming lofty hedge tops. Victorian garden tools like this are worth much more money when the pollen brush, tucked into a hole at the end and once used to fertilise flowers, is still in evidence.

As well as salvage, gardens are often the home of statues. Choose something made of natural stone as it will last longer than man-made alternatives. And remember when you are buying that the appearance of moss or lichen on a statue doesn't necessarily denote great age, as it might be the result of a recent application of yoghurt.

Double Bubble

1. Set of Victorian decorative tiles, made in Staffordshire

    £8 paid, £25 sold

2. Tiffany-style lamp

   £40 paid, £105 sold

3. Pair of cats by retired Stoke potter Lorna Bailey

   £42 paid, £120 sold

4. A redundant, cast-iron public information sign, previously the property of Great Western Railway

   £75 paid, £150 sold

5. A short-handled military shovel, dating from the 1950s

   £25 paid, £50 sold

Analyse That: Makers, Designers and Artists

What's in a name? Quite a few quid when it comes to the value of historic items, says John Cameron.

'There is without doubt a premium to pay on items when you can attach a maker's name to it. I have witnessed areas in twentieth-century English pottery that have, over the past ten years, evolved into major collecting fields. Many of these pieces were once grouped into large lots and sold for very modest sums. After the rise in demand, I bought some useful reference books that traced the development of mid-century pottery factories and provided extensive information on the designers and who they employed. People like a name and, usually, the more interesting or important an artist or designer's contribution to their chosen field, the more documented they will be and thence the greater their celebrity. As a consequence, demand for their work will usually be stronger.'

10

POSTERS AND PICTURES

It wasn't a film for the faint-hearted. According to publicity, the 1940 film *Black Friday* featured stars Bela Lugosi and Boris Karloff 'at their fiendish best'.

The plot was not unfamiliar. 'The sinister hand of science dares a new and dangerous experiment. Into the body of a gentle scholar is grafted the brain of a criminal and a new and deadly monster is born, to ravage an unsuspecting world.'

It was down to poster designs to imply all this, as graphic artists aimed to lure war-time audiences into the cinema with some fiendish behaviour of their own.

In addition to dramatic lettering and the graphic depictions of horror-struck faces, the artists used colour to get their message across. The poster for *Black Friday* was liberal in its use of black, signifying death, as well as a jaundice yellow, for cowardice, and an earthy green, for decay.

'Posters were the only way to promote a film,' explains Charlie Ross. 'The studios wanted people to know what films were about before they stepped into the cinema.'

The film might have remained one of niche interest and largely forgotten, except for the budget home improvements carried out years ago by one former cinema employee in South Wales. To save money and enhance comfort, giant posters like the one for *Black Friday* were stashed under the owner's carpets as underlay. It was decades before they were discovered in a renovation project. At the time, most big-screen posters were thrown away, so at least the ones used as underlay were reprieved, and offered an insight into the way audiences were tempted into the cinema.

This array of posters revealed how the faces and names of major stars loomed large, alongside depictions of action scenes. At an auction in Cardiff, the *Black Friday* poster alone was sold for £1,200, with the entire collection raising £60,000.

Film posters that fall outside of Hollywood's golden era have also sold for large amounts. The hammer came down on one for the 1965 James Bond film *Thunderball*, starring Sean Connery, at £2,200.

But even that pales into insignificance when it comes to one landmark cinema poster purchase. In 2012, a collector paid $1.2 million for nine rare and early posters, with the pick of the bunch being an advertisement for the 1927 German-made silent film *Metropolis*. The film, set in a dystopian cityscape, is considered a high-water mark of early cinema. Among the other posters was one for *King Kong* and another for *The Invisible Man*, both released in 1933. A good number of Hollywood films were made a hundred years ago, thus qualifying the posters as antiques. Given that the life of paper is finite and will deteriorate, there is an ever-diminishing number of older posters in existence.

Today, it's more likely posters relating to much later films will be found for sale and, as with toys, the Star Wars brand is at the forefront of collectors' minds, starting with the trailblazing first of the series, made in 1977.

In 2021, painted artwork for a poster for the sequel, *The Empire Strikes Back* sold for £42,500. 'Star Wars has cult following and it's such a popular subject that prices are high,' explains Thomas Forrester.

Posters publicising vintage British films are still sought after, he says, with *Lawrence of Arabia*, *The Wicker Man* and movies in the Hammer House of Horror genre exciting particular attention. But cinema posters are not the only movie-related artwork pursued these days.

There are billboards that appear on the sides of buses, lobby cards listing upcoming films once handed out in cinema foyers and the posters advertising travelling cinemas that once toured village halls, explains Thomas. All provide good fodder for film buffs.

For Stephanie Connell, there are some stand-out modern classics that create a buzz, including *The Goonies* (1985), *Ferris Bueller's Day Off* (1986) and *Jaws* (1975).

'People who now have a disposable income are buying them for nostalgic purposes,' says Stephanie. Look out for artwork related to limited runs or specific screenings that can enhance value.

Recent films that seem destined to become classics are *Dune*, a bleak science-fiction adventure, and *No Time to Die*, as it was Daniel Craig's last outing as Bond. And posters from these may become sought after by collectors.

If you pick up a film poster that you'd like on the wall, you will need to keep it flat and free from rips, which probably means framing it. If you do, here's Stephanie's advice:

1. Make sure you used acid-free board behind the poster.

2. Choosing glass that shields the poster from UV rays is a must.

3. Don't use glue.

4. If possible, get a professional involved to help keep the poster in mint condition.

Away from the cinema foyer, other posters from bygone eras are sought after, with anatomical posters attracting interest these days.

At the time the artists behind advertising posters were under appreciated, says Stephanie Connell. 'For ordinary people, that is the art they would have seen. They were cheap prints for everyday, busy people who didn't have access to great art.'

Although the first theatre bills were just text, poster art went on to have a proud history. The limitations of lithographic printing were overcome in France at the end of the nineteenth century, and it became the cultural home of the poster, with the most famous featuring the work of artist Toulouse-Lautrec.

Of course, posters with eye-catching pictorial designs were used to advertise all kinds of things, holidays among them. Then came the era of railway posters linked to aspiration, adventures and enterprise.

It's helpful to discern whether a poster is original or a reproduction, and sometimes price is the best barometer. One team looked longingly at a Trans Canada poster, dated 1924 and made to advertise Pacific Hotels and Resorts. When expert Tim Weeks learned the price was £35, he told them it was a reproduction because, he pointed out, an original would likely cost more than £500. If the image was an appealing one, it was probably worth the money, said Tim, although the team ultimately decided against it.

PAINTINGS

Although they're an art form, posters are not art and prices tend to reflect that. Paintings will probably be smaller and more portable and, when it comes to pictures, Raj Bisram has some simple advice for buyers.

'Buy something you like. You are going to hang it on the wall and look at it, possibly for years. If it goes up in value, that's a bonus.

'Condition is always important. Also, make sure it is authenticated. Most famous artists had a school of pupils in their wake, including people like Picasso. Watch out for the phrases that give you a clue about who painted it. Even today's great artists have a team behind them.'

Artist attribution guide

Picasso
Likely to be a work by the artist.

Attributed to Picasso
Probably a work by the artist.

Circle of Picasso
A work by an unknown artist, in Picasso's style and probably painted during his lifetime.

Follower of Picasso
A work by an unknown artist working in the artist's style, who was a contemporary or near contemporary of Picasso.

School of Picasso
A work executed at the time of and in the style associated with Picasso.

Manner of Picasso
A work by an unidentified artist, in the style of Picasso, at a later date but not a recent work.

Style of Picasso
A recent work by an unknown artist inspired by Picasso.

After Picasso
A copy by an unidentified artist of a named work by the artist.

For auctioneers, the story of one artist has dominated the twenty-first century. Once, street artist Banksy sold prints of his work on the streets of Bristol for £35. Now, those same limited-edition prints are selling for tens of thousands of pounds. Richard Madley described 'the Banksy effect' as 'the greatest phenomenon I have seen in my career'.

For him, Banksy is a global 'superbrand', but the artist deserves this pre-eminent position. 'In the world of urban art, Banksy is so far ahead of anybody else.'

Banksy's popularity chimes with modern tastes, Richard explains. 'Today people don't want clutter, and that extends to their wall spaces. They want one signature piece in their room, preferably a great work of art. It's very different to what their parents wanted and there's no longer an appetite for a lot of the stuff I have sold during the past forty years.'

Bargain Hunt's Nick Hall also has a passion for paintings and has watched in dismay as prices for fine Georgian and Victorian work have fallen off a cliff. Paintings by landscape artist Henry H. Parker are a case in point. A decade ago, Nick was selling Parker's rich pastoral scenes, produced in the late nineteenth and early twentieth century for £12,000 or more. At a recent auction, the sale price was just £2,000.

'Today, there are more collectors for modern art,' he explains. 'Work from the twentieth century is in vogue and values are still rising. Even limited-edition prints are selling for thousands of pounds, much more than an original Victorian painting by a Royal Academy artist.'

As well as being an auctioneer, Nick is a valuer who visits houses at the request of the owners to estimate the worth of art on the wall.

'I take with me an eye glass to take a good look at the paintings, and smelling salts, for when I tell the owner how much it is now worth. But if it's worth a fraction of the sum they paid for it two decades ago, at least they have had years of enjoyment from it.'

Of course, markets are cyclical, as Nick points out. 'At some point, we will notice Victorian paintings making a bit more money and it will become a trend, but we don't know if this will be in two to five years, five to ten years or whether it is a thirty-year generational cycle.

'Good Victorian art has never been so inexpensive so it is a good time to build up a collection, hang it on your wall and leave it as an investment for the next generation.'

When it comes to buying a painting, he still believes a canvas is the best option, because at least an oil painting can be restored if necessary. That's a task for a professional conservator who will match colours and even brush strokes to mask the modern touch. And while restored paintings are worth less than untouched originals, they can still find a market.

Watercolours are notoriously difficult to mend if they are ripped and prints must stay crisp and 'as new' or they nose-dive in value. Frames aren't a major consideration. Although an original frame may be preferable, tastes change, as Nick points out, and a buyer may have fixed ideas rooted in the décor of the room in which the picture will be hung.

If you visit an auction and an oil painting catches your eye, it's worth inspecting the back of the picture as well as the front. The way the canvas is attached to the stretcher bars helps to determine its age. In the Renaissance, the bars butted up against one another, or were sometimes held with pegs or even nails. But from the mid-eighteenth century, keys were used to keep the tension tight.

Take the picture from its stand and hold it up to the light. Looking at the back will help to determine if there are any holes in the canvas that will demand a repair. You might also spot tape on the back, which will indicate a repair has already taken place. Such is the market for oil paintings at the moment, damage like this on a Victorian work will reduce its price from £70 to £80, to about £20 to £30.

In addition to Royal Worcester, Philip Serrell has a particular love of pictures and has four tips for bargain hunters:

1. You want to know the provenance of a picture – who painted it and where it has been since it was finished.

2. Watch out for pictures that have been over-cleaned or restored. For example, canvases that have been re-lined behind the original canvas. It's always better to buy something in its original state.

3. Buy the best you can afford.

4. Look out for paintings by craftspeople who later made their names in ceramics. They produced pictures to augment their salary, long before they became well known.

Analyse That: Condition and State of Repair

Original is best, according to John Cameron, and assessing the condition of the item in your sights is crucial.

'A premium will ALWAYS be paid for something in good or original condition and the effect condition has on open-market value will depend largely on supply-and-demand factors. Collectors will accept a certain amount of damage if the item is something that's rare; if they are unlikely to find an example in better condition. Due to the large sums paid for rare items, some sophisticated methods of repair have been developed for all areas of the fine and decorative arts. Anyone buying early and rare football programmes will often be seen holding pages up to the light, to see if tears and hole-punches have been repaired, such is the demand and difference in price for rare programmes in good condition.'

11

ENTERTAINMENT

*A*ccording to Frederick Douglass: 'Once you learn to read, you will be forever free.'

Douglass had fled from slavery and became a respected abolitionist in the US in the nineteenth century. For him, reading was an essential buttress during his incredible journey. It was a cornerstone in his education, as well as being a valued pastime. Today, the free availability of books in shops and libraries is a given and, even in Douglass's time, there were already plenty of books in print.

Credit for that lies with the printing press, a piece of transformative fifteenth-century technology that revolutionised communications. And once it had cranked up, it helped to disseminate ideas and information much more quickly than before. A copy of the Bible became its first major publishing triumph. (Prior to the invention of the printing press, illuminated scripts were handwritten by the minority who knew how, for the few that could read.)

Times have changed. According to UNESCO (United Nations Educational, Scientific and Cultural

Organization), some 2.2 million titles are published worldwide each year. Cosmologist Stephen Hawking once noted that, if new books were stacked next to each other, you would have to move at 90mph just to keep up with the end of the line.

So, given the numbers, it's no surprise to learn that, as an investment, most books aren't worth the paper they are written on. There are, however, a few notable exceptions.

BIG SELLING BOOKS

The world was famously engulfed by Harry Potter fever. But when the first hardback was published in 1997, it was by no means apparent the story would be a hit. As a consequence, the first print run of *Harry Potter and the Philosopher's Stone* numbered just 500 and, of that initial run, 300 were immediately dispatched to libraries. Inside the cover, the book was attributed to Joanne Rowling. Only later was she better known as JK. And there are a couple of printing errors that mark out these early copies from those that came later. On page fifty-three, the word 'wand' is mistakenly included twice in a spell and on the back cover, the word 'philosopher' is spelled incorrectly.

Fast forward more than twenty years and a jumble-sale shopper buys four books for a pound, including a hardback edition of the first Harry Potter story of the series.

Wisely, she took the book to auctioneer Charles Hanson, who quickly pinpointed all the anomalies that this first edition had, as well as a library sticker. It sold for a mighty £28,500.

First editions attract purchasers, while other factors that might add value to books are author signatures and great age.

Best Buy

Small is often beautiful and, running out of time, Gary Pe's team settled for a miniature Bible, costing just £5. Any book less than three inches in length qualifies as a miniature book and these were once favoured by the travelling Victorians for entertainment during long journeys. The title of this one was 'Smallest Bible in the world with Shakespeare's family records in facsimile from the Parish Register Holy Trinity Church Stratford-upon-Avon.' Auctioneer Catherine Southon was impressed by the tiny magnifying lens still tucked into the back of the book. This tiny item attracted a large amount of interest and, when it went under the hammer, produced a bumper profit.

Bought £5 Sold £105 Profit £100

Books were only one form of entertainment prior to the twentieth century. Playing music was another option, although it's notoriously difficult to find antique instruments at today's fairs.

There are some second-hand violins in circulation, thanks to players giving up or going on to better models. Check online for prices before investing and look for a maker's label. At auction, make sure you see and hear the instrument before buying. The same advice, regarding labels and condition, goes for guitars.

An unknown number of parents have hastily dispatched their children's drum sets for sale at the earliest opportunity. If you are tempted by a set of skins, make sure the lugs, tension rods and metal shell are in good shape.

Bargain Hunt teams have experienced mixed fortunes when it comes to buying instruments. One £50 piano accordion made a fat £40 profit at auction after selling for £90. However, a squeeze box hit the wrong note, after being bought for £35 but selling for just £22, perhaps because it looked in need of repair.

TURNTABLES, RADIOS AND RECORDS

Less adept musicians finally had every reason to abandon music practice as a step change in technology changed the face of home entertainment. While its genesis lay in mid-century France, the first recognisable record player was Thomas Edison's phonograph, with its foil-wrapped cylinder, unveiled in 1877. Soon it was modified by Alexander Graham Bell and his superior wax-covered cylinder, which he called a graphophone. However, it was German-American inventor Emile Berliner who finally launched the gramophone in 1887, in which the cylinder was replaced by a flat disc. Commercially made record players, available from 1895, became a feature of homes, distinctive for the giant trumpet from which music blared.

They're the kind of gadget that would attract most *Bargain Hunt* teams, but a purchase comes with a health warning:

1. Always try before you buy.

2. Ensure the correct electrical testing has been carried out before the auction.

3. Invest in a service of all the moving parts.

4. Choose a player with a tin horn, as it sounds better than brass equivalents.

5. Check the turntable speed. There's a mobile phone app that can help with that, which is also useful when it comes to buying more modern record players.

6. Beware of fakes. One way of detecting a phoney is by examining the back bracket. Original models will have sturdy fixings, while fakes are most likely to be flimsy.

The first records were made of shellac and played at seventy-eight revolutions per minute.

Gramophones enjoyed their heyday before being shoved aside by the arrival of radio, after which they were relegated for some years. And after the 1920s, this new invention monopolised the airwaves for some years. Vintage radios are still available today and can be collectible. A 1920s' model undoubtedly has historical value but will it still function? It's a good idea to find out before buying one, while also checking the condition of the casing.

In the 1960s, radios themselves were superseded by record players, with vinyl now entirely taking the place of shellac. Today, it's the vinyl revival that's captured the imagination of many buyers. For those filtering a record collection from their youth, it's not records by the popular bands that make the most money, it's often the lesser bands that sell for more.

One of the most sought-after vinyl records is 'God Save the Queen' by the Sex Pistols. The anarchy linked to the punk movement meant that many of their records were wilfully smashed by fans.

An especially rare copy has fetched £13,000 at auction. It had been recorded by A & M Records. The company dropped the controversial band before the number was released, and most of the copies were destroyed. With the auctioned record in its original sleeve, and the Sex Pistols being the most iconic and infamous punk band, the record was marketed as a piece of cultural history.

However, there are many far more obscure artists that garner attention today, precisely because they are little known and many fewer of their records were released.

Posters and stickers that originally came with records add considerable value. Then there are labelling idiosyncrasies that catch the eye of collectors. Discs released by Island Records depicting a tropical paradise on its core arouse little interest, while the same label using the letter 'i' associated with its branding is highly desirable. As well as rarities and early pressings in good condition, vinyl collectors operate by a series of arcane clues that can be hard to follow. These factors combine to make some Beatles records excel at auction, while others barely register. Auctioneer Colin Young sold two Beatles records in the same sale, with a 33⅓ rpm stereo version of *Please Please Me* selling for £3,400, while a copy of *A Hard Day's Night* went for £6. The values varied so widely due to rarity, condition and provenance. If in doubt, consult an auctioneer for advice.

FILMS AND FILM PROPS

Outside the home, there was one dominant form of recreation, and it was the magic of the moving image.

Even before the arrival of the twentieth century, film reels were already a form of entertainment. Grainy, silent and sepia, they were the preserve of fairgrounds or the end-of-the-pier, with people huddling into a darkened space to marvel at these few moments of footage. In the 1930s, sound and colour arrived to enhance everyone's viewing experience, and soon after that Hollywood reached its golden age, with a prodigious output of full-length feature films. Adoring audiences flocked to see the latest releases and actors became superstars. If studios and their stars were complacent, well, how could they have known how television, which was waiting in the wings, would wreak havoc with people's viewing habits?

Between 1946 and 1960, cinema audiences plummeted by 70 per cent, and by 1984 national cinema audiences had declined to one million a week. Fortunately, cinemas endured and ultimately enjoyed a revival. And this collapse in attendance figures did little to dent the output of film-makers, who could now screen their wares at cinemas *and* on television. Thanks to them, film-related memorabilia has become collectible, with film props a growth market. However, prices are linked to trends rather than great age. Black-and-white films featuring Buster Keaton or Charlie Chaplin are out of vogue, Thomas Forrester explains, and the attraction of screen goddesses like Elizabeth Taylor is fading. 'Film props linked to those films and people like Taylor are not going to make as much money now as they once did as the fan base diminishes,' he says.

However, there's an appetite among buyers when it comes to special effects made prior to the digital revolution for cult films, with Ridley Scott's 1979 film *Alien* being a prime example. In 2020, the Alien's mechanical head sold for £50,000. Made mostly from resin and fibreglass, the head – worn by an actor – has a moveable jaw and a toothed tongue that moves in and out of the mouth. Its resin teeth are coated, so as to look metallic, but behind the fearsome front end there's a gap for operating cables. The model shows signs of wear from use and by virtue of its age. After splashing out on the head, the purchaser also had to foot the costs of transporting it – no small amount when it comes to substantial film paraphernalia.

But it's not the only stand-out prop purchase recently, with Marty McFly's Hoverboard from *Back to the Future* raising a stunning £375,000 at a 2021 auction, and a 'Wilson' ball from the 2000 film *Castaway* making £287,500.

'Buying a prop from a film production is like buying a piece of cultural and social history,' Thomas explains.

'Film has been the new literature for us. Films move people to laughter and tears. It educates and enlightens us, bringing things to the fore which we don't normally see.'

The soundtrack of the *Jaws* movie was enough to stop people going into the sea, and a tessellated clapperboard made for the set in the form of shark's teeth has been sold for £70,000.

Props like this emerge from the 'back end' of the production, via the ranks of backroom staff, or may be given to the stars as keepsakes. The props in significant films still cause a stir today, with auctioneer Catherine Southon bringing the hammer down on one of Willy Wonka's golden tickets at £13,000.

Used in the 1971 film *Willy Wonka & the Chocolate Factory*, starring Gene Wilder, the shiny ticket and its envelope, made from cardboard and foil, enticed the finder to the reclusive confectioner's factory gates with the promise that: 'In your wildest dreams you could not imagine the marvellous surprises that await you.'

The evocative ticket came to auction via a childhood friend of actress Julie Dawn Cole, who played Veruca Salt, who had been gifted it years before.

Television shows also feature familiar props and a Sooty hand puppet is a reminder of when programmes were broadcast in black and white. The original yellow bear had his ears blackened with soot by owner Harry Corbett so he would show up better on the screen, hence the name. Sooty first appeared on television in 1952 and starred in 850 programmes, during which time many puppets appeared on screen. One Sooty puppet used in an early programme was sent by Corbett to a friend as a memento. When the puppet came to auction after being carefully stored for sixty years, it sold for £14,500.

Analyse That: Size and Measurements

Size matters when it comes to the fine and decorative arts world, as John Cameron points out.

'If we consider the valuation and description of an estate agent when describing a house, one would always expect the room sizes to be given, sometimes in both metric and imperial. Measurements can tell us many things about an item, such as age, condition or the potential commercial appeal.'

Shopping at an antiques fair

There's no shortage of choice, but how do you embark on your first *Bargain Hunt*?

1. Find an antiques fair that's being staged near you and work out if there's an entry fee. You can easily find this information online along with details about times.

2. If possible, get a map of the site, which might cover thousands of square metres. Ensure there's a car park and aim to park close to the stalls, in case you buy something big.

3. Before you set off, find out if there's food and drink available at the site. If not, take your own.

4. Turn up early and you will see the best buys as they emerge from stall holders' vehicles. Or turn up late, to buy items people would rather sell cheaply than pack up to take home.

5. Dress for the weather, as there are usually stalls outside.

6. Take cash. Not all stallholders have card machines and few will be inclined to take cheques.

7. If you are an inveterate shopper, set a budget and take time to price up your purchases before handing over the cash.

8. Take a mobile phone. You might be able to look up the objects that interest you online to find out more about them – including an approximate value. If you don't have a signal, ask the stallholder for more information. Most are more than happy to share their extensive knowledge.

9. Take a breath. There's lots to see so give yourself time to make the most of the fair.

'When the sheer volume of items overwhelms you, focus on those cabinets and admire the small wondrous items of beauty,' advises Roo Irvine. 'Small will always be collectible. I always tell myself not to be distracted by the large, the showy, and the touristy. Delve into the areas that people ignore and walk by; that is where the real beauties can be found!'

10. Buy what you like, rather than what you perceive to be an investment. No one knows what's going to be in vogue in the future and, if you can't sell it on, you might have to live with it for a while.

11. Take a tape measure to ensure all your purchases will fit inside your vehicle. If you are planning a spree, consider a trolley to cart them around.

12. Take a magnifying glass or loupe, to scrutinise items, and a torch, to peer into the backs of cabinets.

13. Don't take values from the headline prices on eBay or other online auction sites, warns Catherine Southon. 'That is what is being asked, not necessarily what's being paid.'

14. And check condition carefully. 'Collectors are prepared to pay for the best of the best, and for something rare and unusual,' she says. But if its condition is compromised, the financial worth seeps away.

15. Carry with you a hallmark book, to make the necessary checks when buying silver.

16. When it comes to buying, it's fine to haggle, as business is business. As Mark Stacey points out, the sellers are sometimes pleased to see the back of old stock. 'All dealers are desperate to get rid of some items and may be willing to take a loss, to put the money into something else.' But remember that for stallholders, this isn't a hobby but a job, and the items they are selling are their livelihood. Be respectful and keep smiling as you both reach for the middle ground.

17. Treasure still lies out there, waiting to be discovered. One family had kept a blue-and-white Chinese plate left to them by their grandmother in a drawer for years, until they discovered it would be coveted as a rarity. At auction it sold for £250,000.

12

TWENTIETH CENTURY

The twentieth century arrived with drivers obeying a 14mph speed limit. Before it was over, the fastest vehicle in the world would break the speed of sound.

As people turned their backs on the 1800s, a looming airship drifting above the landscape seemed to foreshadow the future. Yet it was the crisscross of white vapour trails from large and numerous passenger planes that dominated the skies as the century ended.

And the world was thrilled by the prospects in store after Italian pioneer Guglielmo Marconi established transatlantic wireless communication in 1901. At the time, nobody could envisage the computer age that would transform communication in the closing decades of the twentieth century.

On the home front, there were numerous changes from the outset of the 20th century, including the arrival of frozen food, the safety razor, the vacuum cleaner, cornflakes, bras, Brillo pads, penicillin, Tupperware and teabags. The list goes on.

Some of the innovations that indisputably marked the century have appeared on *Bargain Hunt*. The Anglepoise lamp first appeared in the thirties and is a design classic. The man behind it was George Carwardine, originally an engineer specialising in vehicle suspension. Success came after he created a lamp on an arm moved anywhere at fingertip pressure thanks to four springs, offering immense and hitherto unknown flexibility. Demand soon outstripped supply, so he went into business with Herbert Terry & Sons, the company already manufacturing the springs for the lamp. In 1935, the three-spring Anglepoise lamp was unveiled, and since then the design has remained about the same. Originally black and cream, later models came in red, blue, green or yellow. So adaptable were the lights, that they were soon seen in doctors' surgeries, garages and schools and Anglepoise lamps were in production for decades. One *Bargain Hunt* team bought what appeared to be an early prototype for £57. It sold for £85, yielding a £28 profit.

ARTS AND CRAFTS MOVEMENT

With consumerism rampant, it's difficult to tell the story of the century through individual items and much easier to look at eras during which distinctly different styles emerged, which were popular by turns. Today, Bargain

Hunters can allocate more modern artefacts that they find at antiques fairs into one of these clearly defined eras, to better understand their history and value. *Bargain Hunt* presenter Natasha Raskin Sharp reveals everything you need to know, starting with the Arts and Crafts movement, already well established when the twentieth century dawned.

'In mid-nineteenth century Britain – roughly one hundred years after the start of the Industrial Revolution – the factory system dominated the manufacturing landscape,' explains Natasha.

'The country's traditional, rural economy – in which craftsmanship was highly praised – had been sidelined to make way for a financial system driven by mass production and machinery.

'The Arts and Crafts movement rejected this mechanisation; it held craft-based production in the highest regard and it abhorred the inhuman treatment of the men, women and children.

'In 1861, artist and designer William Morris (1834–1896) co-founded Morris, Marshall, Faulkner & Co., a manufacturer and retailer (primarily of furniture) that has become synonymous with the movement. The company's wooden furniture was visibly produced by hand; pigments used to colour textiles were created using natural materials; their artisans were paid a fair wage and worked in suitably safe surroundings.'

William Morris furniture is still in huge demand today, says Natasha.

'Surely the notion that an original Morris chair – with its adjustable back and telltale nicks and notches left by the traditional woodworking tools – was made in an equitable, danger-free environment is a substantial part of the reason that it is worth several thousands of pounds at auction today.

'Arts and Crafts revered and aimed to replicate a medieval aesthetic, one that celebrated what it perceived to be the very expression of integrity: imperfection.'

One indicator of the Arts and Crafts movement was the Design and Industries Association, formed in 1915 with the slogan 'Nothing Need Be Ugly'.

A red team challenged to find an item with a signature on it happened on the sculpted figure of a panther, bearing the Bugatti name. It was a modern, scaled-down version of work by Italian artist Rembrandt Bugatti, brother of the famous carmaker, who died in 1916, aged thirty-one. Still, everyone agreed the animal, on its marble plinth, was likely to see a profit . . . and some fast-paced bidding proved them right!

Bought £85 Sold £450 Profit £365

ART NOUVEAU

Another distinct style with a foot in the previous century unfolded in a slightly later time frame. Dating from 1880, Art Nouveau had a different aesthetic, as Natasha explains.

'The movement known as Art Nouveau (quite literally New Art) represented a stylistic break from what its exponents considered to be "old" and undesirable: mass-produced, indelicate objects synonymous with (and made possible by) the heavily industrialised mid-Victorian era.

'As such, decorative Art Nouveau objects that can be found at antiques fairs up and down the country – lamps, vases, photo frames, plant stands, scent bottles – are relatively easy to identify. Exaggerated "whiplash" curves and undulating organic designs dictate an aesthetic appeal that adds not to the function, but to the form.

'On an Art Nouveau vase, a handle is not just a handle: it could be the stem of an iris; the root of a lily pad; an impossibly long and perfectly placed lock of hair . . . and yet, a handle it remains.

'The branch of an Art Nouveau wall light, typically cast in brass, twists and turns dramatically . . . but the position of the shade and the function of the lamp remain unaffected.

'The aim of Art Nouveau design was to inject an air of theatre where, for decades, it had not previously been found.'

'Find an object from this era that dips and dives and swirls and curves for the sake of design only and there's a good chance you've found a period piece of curvilinear Art Nouveau. Wood, glass, oil paint, metal, ceramic . . . no matter the medium or material, these Art Nouveau objets d'art extol the lack of rigidity found in (and pay homage to) the natural world.'

One *Bargain Hunt* pair went in feet first for a novel umbrella stand from the era, in the shape of a tall, chunky riding or military boot, made by English brassware manufacturers Lombard of Birmingham. The cost was £70, a toe-curling outlay for many. But when it came to auction, the boot returned a £5 profit.

There are different strands within Art Nouveau. The so-called rectilinear style, characterised by straight lines, was perfected by a group of people dubbed The Glasgow Four. They were Charles Rennie Mackintosh and James Herbert MacNair, and their wives, sisters Margaret and Frances Macdonald.

Of them all, it's the work of Charles Rennie Mackintosh that's most celebrated today, not least for the Glasgow School of Art building that he designed, sadly destroyed by fire in June 2018.

Tales from the Auction House

Bargain Hunt expert Roo Irvine has good reason
to recall the Mackintosh name for a purchase she
once nearly made. Says Roo: 'At one particular
auction a few years ago, I placed a "cheeky" bid
on a charming music cabinet, hoping to snap it
up for £100. In the small provincial auction
house we frequented, that was entirely possible.
We weren't able to stay at the auction and left
before bidding started. We called later to see if
we were successful . . . the music cabinet sold for
£36,000! It turned out to be a genuine
Mackintosh piece, and the buyer recognised it
from a drawing in the Hunterian Art Gallery of
a one-off commission for a Mrs Pickering of
Lanark. The lucky new owner then sold it for
£250,000! This true tale is a dream come true
for many Mackintosh lovers and still gives hope
that many undiscovered pieces may still be out
there, waiting to be found.'

Art Nouveau's ripple effect continued throughout the
twentieth century. American artist and sculptor Tom
Bennet, and his twin brother Bob, created sleek, fluid
figures in highly polished bronze in the second half of

the twentieth century. One of them, depicting a dancing woman, was identified by a *Bargain Hunt* duo, who invested £185 in the find. It was a risk worth taking. The artwork – particularly popular in the US – was sold at auction for £440.

ART DECO

The Art Deco style is a truly 20th century one, beginning in 1920 and lasting for about twenty years.

As Natasha explains: 'Unusually, the inception of Art Deco can be pinned down to a specific time and place. As a style, it had been maturing for around half a decade when *L'Exposition Internationale des Arts Décoratifs et Industriels Modernes* (The International Exhibition of Modern Decorative and Industrial Arts) was held in Paris in 1925. Handily, Art Deco is simply a shortened version of the name of that world-renowned showcase of design.

'And while place is certainly a key factor (this began as a distinctly French art movement), time plays a larger part; the outbreak of World War I postponed the exhibition (originally slated to take place in 1913 or 14) for over ten years.

'When the war was declared officially over in 1918 – and as nations grappled with the aftermath of 'the war to end all wars' – Europe's appetite for a new chapter dictated the direction of art, architecture and design.

'So bold was the break from the war-time era of deprivation and devastation that Art Deco objects are (generally) readily identifiable: geometric designs; bold, bright patterns comprising contrasting colours; visual references to travel and transport and speed . . . find an object that matches one or all of these descriptions and it's highly probable that it's a period Art Deco piece designed to usher in a new age of opulence, consumerism and frivolity.'

When it comes to Art Deco the key descriptive words, according to Natasha, are 'serious sophistication'.

'If there's one design that perfectly encapsulates the movement, it's that of the skyscraper. Be it William Van Alen's iconic Chrysler Building, the strikingly tall and architectural 'Skyscraper Furniture' of Paul T. Frankl or any one of the countless decorative objects (coffee pots, clocks, scent bottles, tube radios) that took inspiration from the Manhattan skyline, the message that Art Deco aimed to convey was abundantly clear: the only way is up.'

Mystery Object

The handle was silver, the comb teeth widely spaced, but it was not an implement to untangle the tail of a rocking horse, the best guess among a baffled crowd. This is a cake-breaker, used to slice crumbly sponges more adeptly than knives. It dates from the mid-twentieth century after it was realised that prongs exert less pressure than a blade.

The mid-century was scarred by global conflict, then design underwent another step change, as *Bargain Hunt* expert Stephanie Connell explains. 'The Second World War was an extremely dark time. There were some technological advances rooted in work carried out before and during the conflict that eventually made themselves apparent in the home.'

She highlighted the story of married couple Charles and Ray Eames, whose experiments with plywood during the Second World War led to the use of a new splint for wounded soldiers, which helped prevent gangrene. After the war, they used plywood to make iconic chairs. 'Their work as war-time designers was hugely important and influenced the mid-century design movement,' she explains.

A post-war optimism was then evident, says Stephanie, and there was an appetite for futuristic design. 'It was aspirational and it was fun,' she says. It was the age of consumerism, which was coupled with bigger populations armed with more cash.

The profile of the population in the twentieth century was changing, and that affected the way people spent money. Before the First World War, antique buyers were predominantly wealthy, looking to enhance a country house or London home.

However, between 1901 and 1991, the population of the UK increased by 51 per cent. At the start of the century, the proportion of the population above fifty years old was 15 per cent. Fifty years later, the figure rose to 25 per cent and in 1991, the number was almost one third.

Evidently, infant mortality was declining and people were living longer than ever before. In 1901, baby boys were expected to live for forty-five years, and girls, forty-nine years. As the country welcomed the twenty-first century, those ages were now pegged at seventy-five years and eighty years.

And personal finances had improved. In 1911, one in seven people in the workforce were in professional or management positions. By 1999, that figure had changed to one in three, with many more people spending their disposable income on items from the past.

Worst Buy

When it sped around on the platform of a carousel in the seventies, many lost their hearts to the bright hues of a NASA moon buggy. Decades later, it had the same effect on a couple that splashed out on it as their 'big buy'. But expert Caroline Hawley was concerned it would only sell well in a specialist auction. And she was right, as it inspired just one rock-bottom bid and sold for a tenth of its hefty purchase price.

Bought £200 Sold £20 Loss £180

During the twentieth century, antiques buyers have been joined at fairs by a battalion of collectors, says Stephanie. 'Antiques tend to be individual items while collectibles come in a range and are sought after by completists, a specialist who wants to have a defined set of something that's not necessarily age related.'

The key issues governing collectibles are rarity, condition and that two or more people are competing for items, she explains.

'When you start a collection, you begin to learn a bit more about your chosen area and look out for the item wherever you go. From that starting point, you fall down the rabbit hole and look for rarer pieces. It might be anything from toy trains to street signs.'

When *Bargain Hunt* expert and antiques dealer Mark Stacey reflects on the changes he has seen during his career, he has noted the drop in the number of collectors, although they are being replaced by curious buyers.

'When I first went into business, there were a lot of collectors who focussed on certain items. Today, people don't want to make a collection and choices are usually made with interior design in mind.

'It's lovely to see much younger people coming to antiques fairs, who are really interested in the history of items. One young woman bought a pair of silver-plated grape scissors because she couldn't believe such things had existed.

'And recently, my youngest customer was an eight-year-old who bought a Wedgwood glass paperweight in the shape of a pink rabbit.'

Overlooked and Undervalued

When it comes to finding gems, the twentieth century is fertile ground, according to Gary Pe.

'Production methods changed, people became a bit more creative and there is now an international audience.' Moreover, there's a desire to purchase artefacts in which a personal link is perceived. 'With twentieth-century items, people can look back and remember. There's a psychology to it. When people are buying there may be something inherent in the object that makes them think back, and it forms an emotional connection.'

Around the home, there may be twentieth-century objects that hold no financial value but with a sentimental worth that's priceless.

As a child, Gary spent long holidays on a remote island in the Philippines, in the care of his grandparents. At the knee of his grandmother, with fireflies dancing around them, he heard stories about ancestors and heroes and they ignited in him a passion for the past. From her, he also learned that objects mean much more than just a price tag at an auction, after one day asking why she kept a battered copper vessel that looked fit for the bin.

'This belonged to my mother, your great-grandmother,' she told him. And pointing to a dent in the side, she added: 'It got this after she threw it at your great grandfather after he stayed out late one night and came home drunk.'

The memories and tales that are attached to much-loved items are, says Gary, 'The glory of antiques.'

Double Bubble

1. A Steiff beagle puppy

    £20 paid, £55 sold

2. A sturdy, mid-century bingo game tumbling ball dispenser

    £25 paid, £75 sold

3. A silver, oriental rose water dropper (used for hand cleaning at the table) about a century old

    £40 paid, £90 sold

4. A walking cane with a pommel shaped as a dog's head

    £40 paid, £110 sold

5. A substantial hay knife, made in Sheffield

   £15 paid, £50 sold

6. A set of boxed silver and enamel cup tokens, used to identify a drinking vessel, in the shape of flowers.

   £75 paid, £150 sold

Analyse That: Provenance

Every item has a story and proving the history of an object can make the world of difference to its value, as John Cameron reveals.

'What makes a $1,000 cigar box sell for over $100,000? Being able to say that the cigar box was the former property of John F. Kennedy! It is often very difficult to accurately place a value on provenance, but one thing is for sure, provenance and history will nearly always increase demand. A painting by a well-known artist that had been exhibited and, or, written about in old art journals will usually sell for more than a similar painting by the artist without any history or provenance.'

13

MILITARIA

Heroes come in many shapes and guises, but at least one finished the Second World War at the victory parade in Berlin without a medal pinned to his chest.

It was a rough ride for anyone penned inside a Royal Artillery tank and battling from the French coast, through the Netherlands and the Rhineland and into Germany, as the British Army mopped up resistance from Hitler's still zealous forces in the latter months of the war.

Like other tank crew, Stafford shoe-repairer Tom Matthews choked on cordite fumes, was deafened by the rattle of the on-board machine gun and lived with the perpetual fear of fire engulfing his vehicle. He saw the treacherous countryside and its pockets of enemy resistance slipping by through a forward-facing slit in the tank's metalwork. On-board there was an outsized teddy bear called Tanky, who was Tom's pillow during long, sleepless nights and protector against the sharp points

that protruded inside the growling vehicle on its
bumpy journey.

Four-feet tall Tanky had been a latecomer to the 62nd
Anti-Tank regiment. After leaving England, Tom's tank
stopped at a Dutch village that had been ravaged by
war. There he encountered a woman after her husband
had been arrested by the departing Germans, whose
bombed home had lost all its amenities. So, Tom set
to work and provided for her a stove for heating and
cooking, then located a water supply. Although she
wanted to repay his kindness, most of her belongings
had already been destroyed. But knowing the young
trooper had a three-year-old waiting for him at home,
she alighted on a much-loved teddy, already about
twenty years old and the worse for wear thanks to the
war, and swiftly stitched on two eyes and embroidered
a nose before presenting it to Tom.

The liberation of Europe was no easy feat and Tom
was among thousands put through a gruelling ordeal,
especially after German forces attempted to regroup
with the Battle of the Bulge. Tanky remained by his side,
a comfort when the going got tough. By the time the
tank lined up for the victory parade in Berlin, Tanky was
considered such an important mascot he had pride of
place on Tom's lap.

Finally, when he got home, the Steiff-style bear was
presented to his son, also called Tom. Although he had

been relegated to the loft for decades, Tom Junior didn't want the quirky history to be lost. It was with this resonant wartime heritage that Tanky came to Charles Hanson's auction house. 'The bear is a bit bald or play-worn. Ordinarily, without that rich provenance, it would be worth about £150,' explains Charles. 'But with his backstory on-board the tank, I'm hoping he is going to make four times that amount.'

In fact, the bear exceeded all expectations and was sold for a mighty £4,000. Provenance – the proven background of an item – is key when it comes to enhancing values at auction. Attribution might come in the form of a photo, a form, a newspaper clipping or an official record. With Tanky, it was the story recalled by Tom Junior that stirred so much interest. With some military items, it's relatively straightforward to research the one-time owner and augment the information attached to it.

One example is the memorial plaque issued to the relatives of those who died during the First World War. About 1,150,000 were issued, each bearing the name of the man who had died in raised letters. Also known as a 'death penny', it was made from bronze gunmetal and featured an image of Britannia, an imperial lion, two dolphins denoting British naval power and the words 'he died for freedom and honour' around its rim. With the name, it is possible to cross-reference the Commonwealth War Graves Commission records, which maintains information about First World War victims, as well as their graves. Beyond that, local newspaper reports of the era might furnish further details, which help to build a picture of the dead man and how he died.

Without an enlightening backstory, a soldier's death penny might be worth about £50 at auction, although the value increases if it was issued for a woman. Only 600 were produced to mark the death of females, who were typically nurses.

Where there's a death penny, there should be medals, although often these twin items get parted down the years. The provenance of medals is also pivotal, although at antique fairs it's not always clear who they were awarded to without the appropriate paperwork attached.

'It's important to keep the ephemera attached to medals,' says *Bargain Hunt* expert John Cameron. 'After the Second World War the country was broke, so medals were unnamed and they were presented to recipients in a cardboard box with their names written on them. It is important to keep any associated paperwork, like enlistment papers, certificates, record books and photographs, as they form part of the story that adds value to a set of medals, or other war-time item. It is this information a potential buyer will covet, and then be encouraged to pay a higher price.'

One set of three medals with an unknown history bought by a *Bargain Hunt* team for £26, generated a £14 profit after being sold for £40. But once again, there is no guarantee of profit when it comes to auction.

A different medal dating from the Second World War caught the interest of another team. Its blue-and-white ribbon and monarch's profile indicated it was a Greek medal, issued after the conflict to men who fought on the mainland and in Crete in 1940 and 1941. When first Italy and then Germany invaded the Greek mainland, Churchill was keen to help but he had already directed many of the nation's forces to North Africa. The Greeks and the select number of Allied soldiers diverted there were quickly pushed down to Crete. During a first attempt at invasion, German paratroopers proved easy pickings for entrenched soldiers. Still, Greece's King

George IL was soon evacuated to Egypt, along with all the surviving soldiers.

When this medal was originally issued, it came with a certificate bearing the name of the holder, although on this occasion the paperwork had been lost. On the basis that comparatively few British soldiers were caught up in the action there at the time, it's a medal encountered less often in the UK and, for its perceived rarity, the team paid £33. Unfortunately, the highest bid it attracted was just £22.

By contrast, eleven medals belonging to Royal Navy Commander Gordon Campbell, an acclaimed U-boat killer from the First World War, fetched £840,000 in a 2017 auction. Significantly, a Victoria Cross was among the medals, the highest award for valour.

Steve Nuwar, a dealer in militaria, generates fresh interest in medals as he tries to put names and a history on any that come his way. He discovered one group had belonged to Henry Joseph Bailey who joined the Royal Navy in 1880, aged fifteen. In the early years of the twentieth century, he retired from the Royal Navy and joined the merchant service, and for a monthly salary of £5 10 shillings, Bailey served as master-at-Arms on the ill-fated Titanic, which sank in 1912 on its maiden voyage. Although 1,500 people perished after the four-funnelled ship, dubbed unsinkable by its owners, hit an iceberg, Bailey was one of 712 survivors. He took charge of Lifeboat 16, valiantly urging fifty frightened and exhausted passengers to sing before they were rescued by the SS *Carpathia*. Afterwards, he re-enlisted with the Royal Navy, serving at sea throughout the First World War. He died in 1943 in Southampton, the port city he regarded as home.

Not only did Steve track down this fascinating story but also added photographs of Bailey, distinctive through his walrus moustache, to the medal haul. This rich provenance turned a collection of medals which, had they remained anonymous, were worth no more than, say, £500, into a lot that made a hammer price of £8,500.

Steve was interviewed by Christina Trevanion, who took with her medals won by her own great grandfather, Gerald Arthur Stacey, during the First World War. The Distinguished Service Order and Légion d'Honneur, France's highest award, were, said Christina, 'incredibly cherished' by her family. Gerald died in 1916, leaving a wife and four children, including her grandmother Molly.

Thanks to his research, Steve proved chartered accountant Gerald Stacey was not only a family hero but a national one too, serving as a major in the 2nd City of London Fusiliers. The regimental records say his loss was 'a very serious one. He was a keen and fearless officer, and he was popular with all ranks.'

Moreover, official government records show his family didn't collect the trio of medals he had earned during the conflict prior to his death. At the time, it's likely his widow remained unaware that officers had to claim medals, while for serving soldiers the award was automatically delivered. Gerald's family was marked by tragedy in the Second World War. One of Gerald's sons, Harry, a lieutenant on a Royal Naval submarine, died when his vessel was sunk in 1940. Meanwhile, Christina's grandmother Molly lived to be 108.

John Cameron illustrates how provenance can change the value of a medal group.

'Provenance is like the pedigree one can use to trace an artwork's history or it can almost be like a physical connection to the former owner. One thing is certain, provenance can turn prices on their head and drive bidders to throw caution to the wind and ignore the limit they may have set themselves prior to the auction.'

Several years ago, he sold the medal group belonging to Lionel Peter Twiss. Twiss was a decorated Second World War Fleet Air Arm flier who later earned fame as a test pilot, becoming the first man ever to fly at over 1,000mph in a Fairey Delta IL jet in March 1956. The medal group consisted of a Distinguished Service Cross and Bar, an OBE, 1939–45 Star, Atlantic Star, Africa Star and British War Medal.

'A very nice group but one, after consulting my medal yearbook, I had valued at around £2,000,' explains John. However, alongside the medals were eight pilot's flight logbooks that detailed every flight Twiss had made, including war-time dogfights and his 1,000mph challenge.

'On the day of the auction, several telephone lines had been booked and there were a number of unfamiliar faces in the saleroom – always a good sign! After exceeding the £10,000 mark, two bidders on two separate telephone lines engaged in a dogfight of their own with the hammer coming down at £27,000, more than ten times what my annual medal yearbook had suggested.'

Mystery Object

A letter-sized piece of wood, with a slit down its centre, was distinguished by the engraving of a name, date and regiment. The carved moniker implied it was a personal item. And the slit had a circular hole at one end, which seemed significant. In fact, the biggest clue lay in its link to the Coldstream Guards, where uniforms were kept tip-top. This was a tunic-protector, used when soldiers applied polish to their jacket's brass buttons. The aim was to feed each button through the hole and slide the wooden plank along, so the button could be properly cleaned in isolation, with the fabric beneath shielded. They were made in different shapes and sizes but the personal details inscribed on this one substantially enhanced its value, to an estimated £400.

'Militaria is a vast market,' explains Raj Bisram. 'There's always been a fascination with war, it is in our psyche.'

Certainly, wars have been a recurring theme in British history and one team bought a commemorative coin for £24 dating from the 1730s, marking the naval triumph of a man whose name has largely been lost to history.

Admiral Edward Vernon joined the Royal Navy in 1700, aged sixteen, and within six years had been promoted to captain. The coin was minted after his success in the little-known War of Jenkins' Ear. This was a conflict with Spain that broke out after the Royal Navy Captain Robert Jenkins apparently had his ear cut off in the West Indies. (The severed ear, pickled in a jar, duly appeared before parliament with Jenkins, although he failed to reveal why the traumatic incident occurred.) To restore British pride, Vernon was dispatched, and in 1739 took Porto Bello, in present-day Panama, from the Spanish with six ships. The coin was made, the rousing anthem

Rule Britannia was composed and a London street was named for the triumph, although his defeat by a one-eyed, one-legged, one-armed Spanish commander shortly afterwards has been conveniently overlooked. But Vernon is also recalled for adding water to sailors' rum rations to cut naval drunkenness. As team expert Nick Hall pointed out, the coin was worn, but they placed their faith in coin collectors who buy at auctions. On this occasion, the coin sold for £25, just one pound more than its purchase price, reflecting its eroded faces.

DJ Tony Blackburn purchased a cannon ball for £15 when he took part in a *Bargain Hunt* special and learned how provenance – or lack of it – affected value. Used between about 1698 and 1740, the cast-iron cannon ball had great age but there was little other information that could be discerned about its history. It sold at auction for £20.

TRENCH ART

More abundant than coins and cannon balls, and usually in better condition, trench art is often available at today's antiques fairs, with brass shells transformed into vases probably being the most commonly found.

'Rare items will always make good money and really good examples of trench art are found in museums,' says Raj.

But, while some of the craftsmanship is extraordinary, he warns that the market for trench art is contracting and today it attracts lower prices than previously.

The very name 'trench art' summons up a vivid scene of a mud-splattered, traumatised Tommy finding hard-won solace in his handiwork.

That's a misleading assumption, warns Roo Irvine, as it's actually an umbrella term predominantly linked to the major twentieth-century conflicts that cover a variety of articles.

'Soldiers DID make pieces in the trenches, but they would often be small, such as a ring made of copper or brass, or knives, during relatively quiet periods. Wounded soldiers would take up crafts as part of their rehabilitation. Then there were the prisoners of war. Making trench art became a wonderful way to use quiet time and sell on in order to buy food, cigarettes and the other small pleasures that would make their day more bearable.'

Army workshops were grinding out examples too, says Roo, as well as civilians in the war zone, but these are also comparatively hard to find. Finally, trench art was made on a commercial scale, like any other business.

'This almost strips away the romanticism of it, but bear in mind the tonnes of excess materials needing to go "somewhere". These were sold off by the governments and turned into mass-produced souvenirs."

Even department stores got in on the act after hostilities ended, using spent ordnance as the basis of paperweights and other items, aimed at soldiers who had returned from the front without a souvenir in hand.

It can be hard to distinguish between an artefact genuinely crafted by a serviceman and a raft of mass-produced items. Even engraved names and dates offer no guarantee of provenance.

'A date and location can reveal the conflict, and this is often embossed into the design, or evident on the bottom of the shell case. However, these could be later souvenirs, made to commemorate a battle rather than at it. Instinct and close inspection should help solve the mystery, as handmade pieces often exude a powerful, tangible charm unlike commercial pieces,' advises Roo.

And one *Bargain Hunt* team happened across a late eighteenth-century apothecary's bowl, misdescribed as something fashioned from a World War One mortar shell. The clue lay in its construction. It was made of bronze, which doesn't rust, while shell cases were brass. It was bought for £20 and sold at auction for £60.

The difficulty of provenance is it's not the only part of militaria that makes buyers hesitate. One *Bargain Hunt* team turned down the chance to buy a full Second

World War uniform for £140, fearing its appeal – and size – would be too narrow.

For Philip Serrell, there's an appeal in items that, years ago, were seen on a daily basis but have now fallen under the radar. 'Recently, I bought a badge for £20 that a First World War soldier would have worn on the collar of his suit when he was on leave, which proved he was on active war duty so he wouldn't be given a white feather, the emblem of cowardice that was handed out by women on the streets. Every regiment would have had one to give its men. Given the scale of losses, and the number of men who were chivvied into joining up after receiving a white feather, it's an incredible thought.

'From the Second World War, I have a tin badge given out to those who donated to the Spitfire Fund.'

At the start of the Second World War, Lord Beaverbrook, newspaper publisher and Minister of Aircraft Production in 1940, launched the Spitfire Fund to help pay for aircraft that would defend Britain against a Nazi onslaught. Donations raised through it are thought to have paid for 1,500 planes.

Philip explains the charm of the tiny items. 'I was born less than ten years after the end of the Second World War and when you are brought up with a knowledge of the hardship people lived through, small items like this reveal a lot.'

His joy for these small, emotive items was shared by one *Bargain Hunt* team who bought a cap badge denoting membership of the Royal Flying Corps after they were challenged to find something made of brass. They paid £25 for it, and not only because it ticked a box for them. As fans of militaria, they knew a bit of its noble history.

Little more than a decade after the first manned flight, planes fought in the First World War – and the casualty rate was appalling. The men of the Royal Flying Corps suffered after the Germans invented an interrupted gear that allowed rapid machine-gun fire between the plane's propellers. Although British technology soon caught up, the RFC became known among its men as 'a suicide club'. In April 1918, just six months before the end of the conflict, the Royal Flying Corps became part of the Royal Air Force.

Perhaps in recognition of the sacrifice implicit in the badge, it made £44 at auction, giving them a healthy £19 profit.

The same team bought a Royal Navy sweetheart badge together with a snuff box in the shape of a military cap for £50. The items sold for £75 so, together with their third item, a railway sign that doubled its money, they were golden gavel winners.

Analyse That: Authenticity

The problem of fraud looms large in the modern world, and it's the same story with antiques. As John Cameron points out, education is the answer.

'There have been skilled artists and craftsmen making honest reproductions and outright fakes for hundreds of years. Michelangelo's first big break came after a marble sculpture he made, and passed off as a Roman original, was discovered in the collection of a Florentine Cardinal. In more recent times, Edme Sampson set up a porcelain factory in Paris in 1845 with the sole intention of copying Chelsea, Derby and other well-known European factories.

'"Every day is a day at school." Ask any auctioneer, dealer or collector and they will agree that almost every day you are in this business, you will learn something you didn't know the day before. It is this fact that maintains and fuels our interest.

'If you are completely new to antiques, I would suggest that you first obtain some general reference books or one of the many decorative art dictionaries available containing good descriptions of the fine and decorative arts. Read them as much as possible and travel to auction houses, museums, fairs and dealers' shops to observe and handle items whenever the opportunity arrives. If you have a particular interest, purchase the best specialist reference book you can afford and start reading. Most will usually contain a "Glossary of Terms" so you can familiarise yourself with the terminologies of your chosen subject.'

14

SPORT AND GAMES

Love it or hate it, for many, football is England's national game. Its roots may well lie in woaded warriors kicking the severed heads of their vanquished enemies around a battlefield. In fact, it wasn't until 1863, after the launch of the Football Association, that unseemly tactics like gouging and biting were outlawed. Times have changed and today there are 40,000 registered clubs in England. So, it's no surprise to learn that many devoted football fans collect football ephemera and sometimes high prices are paid for the privilege.

FOOTBALL MATCH PROGRAMMES

Match-day programmes are one example and, once again, it is scarcity that pushes up prices.

According to *Bargain Hunt's* Tim Weeks, there is, broadly speaking, a date-line that's key. In 1955, British prime minister Winston Churchill resigned on the grounds of ill health, the polio vaccine was declared safe and

Cardiff was proclaimed the capital of Wales. Any match brochures dated prior to that year might ignite the interest of today's collectors. Afterwards, there's a significant downturn in a programme's worth.

'Programmes from the 1920s and 1930s are rare,' explains Tim. 'People didn't tend to keep memorabilia back then. In fact, there were programme bins at the exits. With the Second World War, there was a shortage of paper, so few programmes were produced.

'For some matches, the programmes still in existence may number in the tens rather than the hundreds. Today, these are beautiful bits of social history, about the club you love.'

For once, it's not the big clubs that are associated with the fattest auction prices. 'A programme from the match between Chelsea and Arsenal in 1948 would be worth £8 at the most. One from a game between Bath City and Yeovil Town is likely to fetch at least three times that.'

After England won the World Cup in 1966, more people than ever before started football-related hoards, meaning items from the era are much easier to come by.

Today, the record for a football programme sale stands with an FA Cup final meeting between the Old Etonians and Blackburn Rovers, held at the Kennington Oval on 25 March 1882. In 2013, it went under the hammer for £35,000. But any from the first half of the century are likely to excite some interest and may well be the very publication a collector needs to complete a set.

SUBBUTEO

As well as programmes, there's Subbuteo, the finger-flicking table football game invented by a British ex-servicemen in 1946. It's set up like a real game, only in miniature, and the original has cardboard figures attached to a chunky button and weighed down by a lead weight. In 1961, the playing figures became three-dimensional and the popularity of the game soared. Now, the appeal for collectors is to have less common teams in their dated kits. Tim Weeks admits to having 200 teams in different strips and is delighted to have recently acquired a Plymouth Argyle team at a cost of £99. Again, the big names don't attract the cash, Tim explains. It's the smaller clubs and countries on which the most financial value is placed.

When it comes to football ephemera, the ball itself seems an obvious choice. Yet significant or signed balls are not necessarily the centrepiece owners might hope for, as they deflate and the signatures on them can fade.

Still, a football from 1982 signed by the Tottenham Hotspur team when it was managed by Keith Burkinshaw and featuring the name of star striker Glenn Hoddle tempted *Bargain Hunt* celebrity team John Watson and Manish Bhasin. Although it looked a bit deflated, the pundits knew that Tottenham had a strong army of supporters who would relish the opportunity to buy just such a memento. And thanks to their instincts, they scored, with the ball selling for £140 at auction, making a £102 profit.

Tales from the Auction House

In 2017, the first contract signed by football legend Sir Stanley Matthews sold for more than £4,000. It revealed the star was paid £5 a week when he signed with his home team, Stoke City FC, in 1932. A second contract found later showed that by 1935 Matthews was on £7 a week, and £8 if he played for the first team, and it sold for £3,100. The paperwork had been kept in a drawer after being given to a local man in exchange for a debt.

CRICKET MEMORABILIA

Richard Madley agrees that football ephemera tops the table at auction. 'Stepping down in the pecking order, cricket would follow football in terms of sporting memorabilia collected globally. Predominantly, the collectors are people who love cricket played by England and Australia and, when it comes to an historic bat or ball used in an important match, there's a great bidding rivalry between the two nations.'

A lifelong cricket fan, Richard used to conduct player auctions for the Indian Premier League, where he is known as 'Hammer Man'.

In 2022, photos, programmes, kit and trophies gathered by Hampshire and England cricketer Derek Shackleton went to auction. A long-sleeved sweater he wore while playing for Hampshire sold for £50; a cricket ball mounted on an oak stand marking his 2,500th first-class wicket went for £190; and a county cap and two ties were auctioned together and raised £200. An autograph book signed by cricketers of the early part of the twentieth century and found in a dusty suitcase in agarage in Bath sold for nearly £15,000.

Beyond cricket comes golf, although here Richard sounds a note of caution.

'There should be a government health warning, that the value of goods can go down as well as up.'

Thirty years ago, prices for golfing memorabilia were booming, he explains, with enthusiastic collectors in America, Japan and Spain leading the charge. 'The market needs new blood now to keep it active, and there's no sign of it so far,' he warns.

After golf, rugby and tennis are next in a descending order. After that comes fishing, a surprise sporting candidate perhaps but split cane rods and brass reels signed by eminent makers attract interest at auction, he says.

CIGARETTE CARDS

Before the age of television, children saw the faces of their sporting heroes and their sports kits on cigarette cards, avidly collected and swapped in the quest to achieve sets. Initially, the card put inside flimsy cigarette packets to make them more robust was blank. In time, manufacturers used advertising on these 'stiffeners', which finally morphed into sets of cards, with Liverpool-based Ogden's the first company to produce collectible cards in 1894.

It wasn't just football and cricket players that appeared on cigarette cards. The subject matter extended from kings and queens and cars to flowers and birds and, for their pictures and the information provided on the back, the cards were dubbed 'the working man's encyclopedia'. But it was the cards featuring the sporting legends that caused a frisson among fans.

In 1907, James Taddy & Company issued no fewer than 595 different footballer cards with its cigarettes. A year later, a sixty-card set featuring the captains of different football clubs was issued by Cohen Weenan, a small tobacco company based in London. In Manchester in 1928, J. A. Pattreiouex included seventy-five different cards as part of the Cricketers Series, with their Senior Service cigarettes. Today, the early sports cards achieve considerable value for something that effectively cost original collectors nothing.

One game beloved by children for centuries is marbles. In ancient times, children rolled small clay balls for sport. By the twentieth century, marbles were made of glass, and you don't have to be a 'mibster', or player, to appreciate how tactile and attractive marbles can be. The older and most rare ones are hand blown and they bear a pontil mark, revealing where they were joined to the molten glass being used for production. A single nineteenth-century handmade marble might be worth as much as £100. Machine-made marbles are smoother but might also be collectible for their exquisite patterns. There are onion skins and oxbloods, cat's eyes, corkscrews and clearies, and numerous others to delight a marble enthusiast. The game – which had different rules depending on where in the country it was being played – was widely enjoyed in the 1930s, then had a revival in the 1970s. If you are buying, watch out for chips and scratches picked up during play.

Another outdoor activity, once popular but now largely obsolete, is model yacht racing. First made as trials for real boats, model yachts became popular in Victorian times when parks cropped up in Britain's towns and cities, usually with a pond as their heart. One *Bargain Hunt* team that seized on a wooden, kit-built boat was concerned the £85 purchase price was high. But when the hammer finally came down, it sold for £120.

Mystery Object

At first glance, anyone wielding a pair of long, fat beechwood sticks with bulbous ends would seem to have malicious intent. In fact, these are Indian clubs, used for exercise in Victorian times. Users could choose stirring activities from books published at the time, with titles like *Manly Exercise*. Club swinging was twice picked as an Olympic sport before the Second World War. Thought to be Hindu in origin, clubs like these are worth about £50 now.

There are various strategy games that can be played inside that have kept adults and children spellbound down the decades, such as Chess.

Tales from the Auction House

Roo Irvine relates a story about unprecedented value being attached to a single chess piece after it found its way to auction in July 2019.

'The owner's grandfather, an Edinburgh antiques dealer, bought the chess piece for £5 in 1964. Not knowing what it was, the family kept it due to its unusual 'magical qualities' and the unusual looking chess piece sat in a family drawer for fifty-five years. Although just 3.5 inches high, it sold for an incredible £735,000. These are the fairy tales we all hope to stumble across in our own homes. Easier said than done, might I add, but these "finds" are still being found!'

Best Buy

A French-made chest containing rainy pastimes, including chess, solitaire and roulette, proved to be a sure-fire bet for one 2003 team, who were dazzled by its possibilities. With a label revealing the makers were based in the Rue de Louvre, Paris, expert Thomas Forrester called it 'a games compendium of magnitude'. The bidding, carried out live on television, thrilled a packed auction house.

Bought £230 Sold £750 Profit £520

There are plenty of wooden sets to choose from, the most elegant being associated with the long-established Stauntons brand, in boxwood or ebony. The name was taken from nineteenth-century English chess master Howard Staunton, although the pieces were made and promoted by Nathaniel Cooke, who had links with the games-maker John Jaques.

As a rule of thumb, Richard Madley advises the taller the chess piece, the more valuable it is likely to be, and if the pieces are stamped or signed by the maker, so much the better. In 2021, an early Staunton chess set, dating from 1849 and with a Gothic casket to store the pieces, sold for £4,600. It was defined by a paper registration label that featured Staunton's signature. The lot had a guide price of between £150 and £200.

Bridge remains a popular game and one *Bargain Hunt* team seized the chance to buy a 1905 set containing not only cards but four hallmarked silver pencils as well. The lid of the box was also framed in hallmarked silver and the cost was a tempting £75. When it went to auction, the hammer came down at £90.

Bagatelle boards are an echo back to the nineteenth century, when a table game derived in France gained more universal popularity. In their most rudimentary form, a ball bearing is propelled by a spring around a course defined by a pattern of metal pins. Today, bagatelle boards are appreciated by collectors like Richard Madley, who has helped to re-purpose them and other distinctive games.

'I like bagatelle boards and I buy them myself,' he explains. 'They are almost pieces of folk art. While they won't be used again for their original purpose, a group of them looks great on a wall. I've done the same with dartboards. You can pick them up at car boot sales for very little money. The older and more well used they are, the better. One wall with twenty to thirty boards on it – perhaps in a restaurant or shop – looks sensational for a small cost. It just needs the interior decorators' market to buy into the idea.'

Five Golden Gavels

It isn't often that *Bargain Hunt* presenters give out a clutch of golden gavels at the show's end. But presenter Charlie Ross found himself distributing five of the highly desirable accolades after the two teams and their experts went head-to-head in Wetherby, Yorkshire.

Red team Janette and Rob, challenged with finding something from the coast, invested £20 in a shipwright's tool. Auctioneer Caroline Hawley dated it to the end of the eighteenth century because, she said, later examples had a corkscrew mechanism, which this one lacked.

Under the guidance of Charles Hanson, they next bought a set of Victorian scales in immaculate condition for £130. Also dating from the Victorian period, their third purchase was a delightfully decorated hollow wooden ball which, the stall holder explained, was attached by ribbons to a woman's wrist to neatly hold wool or thread while she was crafting.

The scales sold for a mighty £210, while the hammer price on the wool holder was £50. With the shipwright's tool achieving £50, they peaked with a profit of £150. Unfortunately, the amount was dented by the Art Nouveau pendant Charles presented as his bonus buy, which sold for a £45 loss. (The team chose to go ahead with the bonus buy, secure in the knowledge that their golden gavels were safe.) But they still had £105 of profit to their names.

Meanwhile, the blue team, Daniel and Robynn, fell in love with a table made in their home town of Leeds. Its wooden legs fulfilled the challenge, to buy something made from a natural material. As they toyed with two Georgian tea caddy spoons, *Bargain Hunt* expert David Harper suggested buying both for £120, although it was the 1810 silver spoon made by Birmingham silversmith Samuel Pemberton, with its mother-of-pearl handle, that caught Caroline Hawley's eye. Their final buy was a set of six Royal Doulton character jugs, items that Caroline acknowledged were 'well past their sell-by date'. Robin Hood and King Henry VLs were among them, but it was the presence of 'Old Charley', familiar as one of the original character jugs, that made the £36 price tag worthwhile.

When it came to the auction, the table sold for £175, the spoons for £150 and the toby jug selection for £38. A solid silver snuff box, made in Edinburgh in 1891 and bearing hallmarks on both lid and base, was David's bonus buy. Even though it made a £5 profit, the blues total of £72 still wasn't enough to catch the rival reds. But all the contestants went home with brass in their pocket and a golden gavel on their lapels. David also received a golden gavel and it was only Charles Hanson who left empty-handed.

15

CLOCKS AND WATCHES

*A*mong the milling crowds on London's city centre pavements, the face of a middle-aged woman in dark clothing was almost hidden by her hat. It was the early decades of the twentieth century and her mission was a vital one. Thanks to her, accurate time was delivered to watch and chronometer makers across the capital.

Ruth Belville, known as the Greenwich Time Lady, was continuing a family tradition. When her father John started the business, years before, most people whose business relied on accurate timekeeping were compelled to knock on the door of the Royal Observatory at Greenwich.

In 1833, one of the first public timekeeping devices came into commission in London: the Greenwich Time Ball. At 12.55 pm, the ball would start to rise to the top of its mast. Ships' navigators trained their telescopes on it, waiting for it to drop at the stroke of 1 pm. This pinpoint accuracy was all very well for shipping but most of London's time piece manufacturers work out of sight of the Time Ball.

In response, John Henry Belville, an assistant working at the Observatory, set his pocket watch against the master clock there, before once a week setting off around London to distribute the accurate time among businesses in Clerkenwell and its environs, who paid for the weekly service by subscription.

The case for accurate timekeeping became all the more pressing with the age of the railway. Until then, outlying areas took their time from the position of the sun. However, there was a marked difference between midday in, say, London and Bristol, which implied there could be chaos for travellers and train companies alike. In 1840, times were standardised, permitting the adoption of a national timetable and the safe use of single tracks. The electric telegraph developed alongside the maze of railways that spread across the country. Yet this new real-time technology did nothing to diminish the demand for Belville's services. He continued on his beat for twenty years until his death, when his widow Maria stepped in at the request of his customers. When she retired in 1892, in her eighties and partially blind, she had 100 subscribers – people who felt that modern methods still could not be trusted, and who enjoyed the human interaction her visits brought.

Now the mantle passed to their daughter Ruth, thanks to the cooperation of the Astronomer Royal. It was forty-eight years before she retired, also in her eighties, but not before the family had provided 104 years of continuous timekeeping in the capital. Her route led her from the city to Kensington, and between Baker Street and Chelsea, and she mingled unnoticed with businessmen and hawkers alike. Her client list eventually dropped to about fifty, after she encountered considerable competition, not least from improvements with new technology. Finally, she gave up work when the outbreak of the Second World War presented too many personal dangers. When she handed her chronometer back to the Royal Observatory, it was found to be only one-tenth of a second out, even though it was made at the end of the eighteenth century. Since her father's day, it had been well maintained at the Royal Observatory.

From 1936, one of Ruth's main competitors was the talking clock, known as Tim. This was available to anyone with a telephone and was instituted because the 15,000 telephonists employed by the General Post Office fielded 26,000 calls a week from people asking the time. Employee Ethel Cain became known as the 'the girl with the golden voice', and she enjoyed a twenty-seven-year spell as the country's chief time-teller. Four discs held in a large machine contained the recordings of her giving the hours, minutes, seconds and the familiar phrase 'at the third stroke, the time will be . . .'. After she had been picked as the voice for the talking clock, a technician realised the gap in her teeth would produce an audible hiss for callers and spent a year painting out the unwelcome sound effect on the discs.

Today, accurate time keeping is taken for granted. But the origin of clocks and watches, although it preceded Ruth Belville by some margin, isn't embedded in ancient times. Certainly, there were devices in classical civilisations that helped tell the time. Sundials were among them, but obviously were no good at night. Water-driven clocks were fine unless there was unduly hot weather, when the water might evaporate. At the time, the concept of seconds, minutes and hours remained alien. By the end of the Middle Ages, Europeans were devoting considerable efforts to tame the tricky issue of timetelling.

The basis of the mechanical clock was created as early as 1275, powered by heavy weights and friction. By 1386, a faceless clock was installed at Salisbury cathedral, striking the hour (which was all that was needed to call the local population to prayer).

The next step was to include a clock face and reduce the scale of clock mechanisms, or escapements, so they could be incorporated into homes.

While a series of springs helped to refine timekeeping, it was the introduction of the pendulum in the mid-seventeenth century by Dutchman Christiaan Huygens that nailed the design, drawing on principles set down by Galileo in the previous century. It was only a matter of time before cathedral clocks were reduced to wrist-watch size, and society became governed by time.

Today, the wristwatch market is a huge base for collectors, says Stephanie Connell. 'In the past ten to fifteen years the market has boomed and prices are stronger. Watches are usable antiques or vintage statement pieces. They are an investment but also wearable. They are linked to technology, history, rarity, luxury brands.'

Danny Sebastian is once again in agreement with Stephanie, saying, 'One of the best and biggest investments for the future is a wristwatch. They have really come into their own recently, especially for men. The market is going up, up, up.'

Top names like Omega, Rolex and Swiss-made watches are among the best investments, he advises, but adds that more prolific brands like Seiko and Timex are also keenly priced now.

Using the example of wristwatches, Danny says an interest can turn into a tidy profit. 'If you are savvy and you buy right and buy quality, this hobby will mean you have items that go up in value and that you love. It's a win/win.

'The key to it is go with your heart and it is going to work for you.'

Still, stories of fortunes unexpectedly made through an apparently common-or-garden wristwatch warm the heart. One bought from a jewellers on Derby Road, Nottingham, in the 1970s sparked a bidding war when it went under the hammer in 2018, eventually selling for more than £50,000. For years, the Tudor Rolex steel Oysterdate had been worn by its owner as he worked on his allotment, so he knew when to return home for tea. Before the sale, auctioneers had estimated its likely sale at just £5,000.

Today, buyers are keen on 1970's Omega watches with stainless-steel cases. Look for Constellation and De Ville models, which are midsized so they can be worn by men and women. To maximise value, choose watches with the original box and papers. Still, one *Bargain Hunt* team drawn to a watch that didn't come in a box paid £100 for it. At auction it sold for £190, bringing the pair £90 profit.

16

CHRISTMAS

Typically, Christmas is a time of eating, drinking and being merry. But, rather than measuring festive pleasure by the pint, the way most of us find joy in the season is linked to what we recall of Christmases past. From the decorations on the tree to the Nativity, it's impossible to celebrate Christmas without casting a nostalgic look back at family rituals held dear from childhood.

Perhaps it was this that fuelled the auction price for three small, porcelain Santas that spent untold years decorating yuletide cakes on the continent after the turn of the twentieth century. A *Bargain Hunt* team delighting in Christmas-themed purchases paid £50 for two items – two Santas together on a sleigh and a reclining Father Christmas figure. The particular tone of the red suits and their patina was enough to take the team on a sentimental journey after they spied the Santas at an antiques fair. At auction they got their reward when someone else, inspired by evidence of the Christmas traditions from a century ago, paid £55 for them.

Christmas hasn't always centred around a Santa and the sackful of presents that he traditionally brings. Our red-coated roof-top rider is a relative newcomer, although celebrations in the middle of winter are long-established, with December celebrations part of Roman life long before the time of Christ. Called Saturnalia, for the Roman god Saturn, it was at these celebrations that luxury imported foods like pine nuts, dates and figs were distributed both to soldiers and among households.

By medieval times, Christmastide, as it was called, was a firm fixture on the calendar, with the name Christ's Mass first appearing in the records in 1038. However, at the time Twelfth Night – the end of the twelve days of Christmas and celebrated on either 5th or 6th January – played a more prominent role in celebrations than it does today. The practice of bringing evergreen foliage into the home for decoration was started, as were Christmas games – although they might have been considerably more boisterous than those we play today.

As for food, mince pies were a fixture, but not as we know them. The pies were made with meat and featured three spices – cinnamon, clove and nutmeg – to reflect the three gifts of the Magi. The best available meat was funnelled into pies that were eaten by the wealthiest in society. Animal scraps, like the heart, lungs, liver and kidneys, were presented to the servants and poorer people, and they made umble pie. (That's presumed to be the root of the phrase 'to eat humble pie', for its association with the lowliest in society.)

In the Tudor age, Christmas plays became popular – as did sugar. The Elizabethan court held sugar banquets to celebrate the season, and ultimately the Queen's passion for it caused her teeth to rot.

There was a change of tenor when the Puritans got the upper hand during the English Civil War. Keen to have Christmas, Easter, Whitsun and every Sunday as quiet times devoted to the contemplation of sin, Parliament passed a law that effectively outlawed the traditional mid-winter holidays. It resulted in riots across the country. Finally, the law was all but ignored until the Restoration in 1660, which scrapped the ruling.

But it was in Victorian times that Christmas came of age. In 1843, just six years after the Queen came to the throne, Charles Dickens published *A Christmas Carol*, revealing through his social commentary that the occasion already merited a public holiday, a family meal and even parties for some.

In the same year, Sir Henry Cole commissioned an artist to create the first Christmas card. Cole was an influential figure in society, as an inventor, educator and patron of the arts, among other things. As such, he found himself inundated with mail, and hit on the idea of a card to simplify his communications.

Roo Irvine explains: 'He commissioned an artist friend, J. C. Horsley, to create a design that Cole had in mind – a family enjoying Christmas (controversial, as the children had glasses of wine, and that didn't sit well with the temperance movement).

'This simple decorative card could easily be personalised with the sender's name. A thousand cards were printed but were expensive at one shilling each. The venture flopped, but the first Christmas card was born.'

Thanks to the arrival of the halfpenny post, and the fuelling of Christmas traditions by the continental habits of Queen Victoria's husband, Prince Albert, cards became an integral part of the commercialisation of Christmas and began selling in droves. Of course, Cole's original ones are now highly sought after, as Roo explains.

'Only twelve of the original cards are said to survive out of a thousand. One example sold at auction in 2001 for a record £22,500. It wasn't just a Christmas card; it was a piece of history borne of human need, sentimentality, the technological revolution and, most importantly, the magic of Christmas.

'The iconography used in the cards makes them so special and stokes the festive fire in our hearts. Early

Victorian cards featured nativity scenes, but then progressed to snow scenes and robins.'

There's a troubling side of Victorian cards that has thankfully been lost to history, as Roo elaborates.

'The Victorians had a dark sense of humour – some cards featured bloodthirsty snowmen, demonic bats, dancing insects, and even Satan popped up too! (The anagram isn't lost on me there!) There's even Santa shoving a naughty child into his sack to steal!

'There are many modern reprintings of Victorian designs, but to find an original is quite rare indeed. They are a thing of beauty, hand painted and coloured, on delicate lacy paper with sumptuous illustrations.

'Receiving one of these in the post 150 years ago would have been a joy and I'm sure they ended up preserved in Victorian scrapbooks as opposed to thrown in the bin as we do.

'The irony goes full circle when you realise that Christmas cards were created as a time-saving idea and yet today, we don't have the time to send them! Ecards became our generation's time-saving invention, and now often a text will suffice.'

Four years after the first cards came another couple of Christmas benchmarks. British confectioner Tom Smith came up with the idea of a cracker, mostly as a way of merchandising his bon-bons. Later the sweets were replaced with gifts and paper hats.

The following year the *Illustrated London News*, a significant journal of the day, published a drawing of the Royal Family celebrating Christmas around a tree. Prince Albert brought with him from his native Germany the tradition of a tree that would be lit with candles and before long, British homes adopted a similar convention, putting small, unwrapped toys on tree branches to the delight of children on Christmas Day. This indicated a calendar change as previously New Year or beyond had been seen as a more appropriate occasion for gift giving.

It was this same German influence on the Royal Family that introduced plum pudding to the festivities. Made some weeks prior to Christmas, the kitchen came alive for 'Stir-up Sunday, the last Sunday before Advent, falling at some time towards the end of November. Traditionally, there would be thirteen ingredients, symbolising Jesus and his disciples, and the mixture would be stirred from east to west, to reflect the journey of the Magi.

Festive puddings were brightened up by the addition of silver charms, another ritual thought to have been inspired by Queen Victoria. Each charm had a message for the finder: there was a coin for good fortune, a horseshoe for luck and a thimble for thrift.

Christmas celebrations continued to evolve, with turkey coming onto the Christmas menu thanks to Edward VLs, who professed it was his favourite. But inevitably, the global conflicts that arose in the first half of the twentieth century cast a gloomy shadow.

It was thought that soldiers jubilantly cheered as they made their way to the Western Front in August and September 1914 would be home by Christmas, to celebrate with their families. The sense of disappointment when that hope did not materialise must have been huge, especially as the number of deaths was already mounting.

That first Christmas of the war, British and German soldiers orchestrated an unofficial ceasefire on Christmas Day, to sing carols in their trenches and play football in no-man's land. It also saw a Royal initiative help to make soldiers feel a little closer to home.

Although only seventeen, Princess Mary, the only daughter of George V and Queen Mary, began a national campaign to provide Christmas gifts for the troops. The present was a brass tin, with her profile on the lid, containing assorted home comforts, like tobacco, chocolate and matches. There was also a card from her, with her picture on the front and inside bearing the words: 'From Princess Mary and friends at home'. As unprecedented rainfall soaked the soldiers and turned their earth-dug trenches into a nightmarish quagmire,

355,000 tins were dispatched from the UK. And as the war continued, so did the Princess's Christmas Fund, supplying 2.6 million tins before the conflict's end. After the war, she received a letter from one veteran who told how he was using the box to store personal items and was carrying it in his uniform's top pocket when it deflected a sniper's bullet. As the tins became commonplace, an empty one might raise about £30 at auction today. Much rarer are tins with the original contents inside, which would have a value that extended to three figures.

In 1915, Christmas did little to lift the national mood, with the disastrous Gallipoli coming to an end after ten months. While the evacuation of troops and equipment under the cover of darkness went smoothly, the episode had cost 25,000 lives, and three times that number were wounded. But the main cost was in sickness, which rampaged among the troops, with 96,000 men admitted to hospital. The following year, the nation spent Christmas mourning the victims of the Battle of Verdun, and even in 1917, it was clear soldiers were rooted at the front line for some time yet, with no apparent progress being recorded.

However, the festive seasons still unfolded at home, even if celebrations were muted. By now, Norway spruces were the Christmas trees of choice. And boys would be hoping for a set of lead soldiers on Christmas morning, or other military models that chimed with the war effort, while girls might favour a porcelain, bisque, wooden or rag doll, depending on household income.

Within a few more decades, Christmas celebrations had changed again, with paper chains strung from the ceiling and artificial trees finally gaining traction over freshly cut ones.

The first Royal radio Christmas broadcast came in 1932, with King George V reading words written by journalist and author Rudyard Kipling. Speaking from Sandringham, the King opened with the lines: 'Through one of the marvels of modern science, I am enabled, this Christmas Day, to speak to all my peoples throughout the Empire. I take it as a good omen that Wireless should have reached its present perfection at a time when the Empire has been linked in closer union. For it offers us immense possibilities to make that union closer still.'

After his father's death, George VI broadcast at Christmas 1937, although it was not an annual tradition for him until the war. While he was speaking on the radio, the fledgling BBC television service broadcast 'the National programme', in effect a musical interlude that gave viewers the opportunity to tune in on the radio. At the time, there weren't many televisions in Britain and only a few hours of programming were broadcast each day, watched on a flickering small screen.

Television technology had developed in the late 1920s and the BBC began transmitting services in 1930. By 1938, television sets, which cost about thirty-five guineas, were still uncommon, with only an estimated 20,000 across Britain. More likely, people played games like charades, consequences and hunt the thimble. Some households had access to Scrabble and Monopoly. After the Second World War, televisions were starting to crop up in people's homes, so were electric fairy lights for the trees, and baubles.

Christmas decorations still bring immense joy to young and old alike, and many sets have been cherished for generations. Yet, although everyone has their own favourites, not everyone is a winner. And, as if to prove it, an auction room failed to fall in love with the dozen vintage baubles in their original compartmented box, bought in a *Bargain Hunt* Christmas Special for £38. The highest bid came in at just £32.

Economically, though, times were tough for many between the wars and, while stockings put up at the hearth might have been filled with nuts and an orange, there was often little by way of toys or other goodies. For some, the season went without a bang.

Caroline Hawley unearthed a boxed set of twelve crackers dating from the 1930s, in three different colours of crepe paper, each decorated with the paper image of a dwarf. Walt Disney's popular cartoon *Snow White and the Seven Dwarfs* – the first full-length animation ever made – came out in 1937, so at the time the imagery was on-trend. To the delight of her team, the bonus buy made a £30 profit, after reaching a hammer price of £55.

It was in the thirties that the character and appearance of Father Christmas was at last settled. His roots lay in St Nicholas, an early saint who was celebrated in various forms for centuries. Each country had their own version of him, with different names and faces, but usually draped in green robes.

When Clement Clarke Moore wrote his poem 'The Night Before Christmas' for his children in 1822, he described St Nicholas as 'a right jolly old elf' and revealed that his mode of transport was a small, reindeer-powered sleigh. The image summoned up by those words was turned into cartoon form by Thomas Nast some fifty years later and was published in *Harper's*

Weekly. Nast's pipe-smoking, present-laden Santa of short stature became an enduring caricature. However, it was after the image was appropriated by large corporations for advertising purposes that the scarlet-robed, white-bearded figure that's familiar today became the accepted motif for the season. A French chocolate mould dating from the 1940s and reflecting Santa's image of the era was a sweetener for one team and they ended up paying £42, but selling for £75.

With the Second World War, families were once again parted from servicemen and in 1939 many children had been evacuated, spending Christmas in rural homes with host families. Christmas spreads everywhere were beset by shortages, with substitutions necessary for key ingredients in the cake and pudding. A year later, and many people's homes had been wrecked in sustained bombing campaigns. In 1941, the shortages extended to Christmas paper, so presents were given unwrapped. Cards were made of flimsy paper and the post office struggled to find staff to carry out deliveries. America entered the war that year, and afterwards US soldiers based in Britain joined families for the festive season. Some lucky children received gifts handmade by their servicemen fathers when they were off duty, or presents from America, via GIs.

At the end of the conflict, a new era unfolded, imbued with optimism. With economic recovery, more

households had televisions, either rented or bought.
In 1957 it was down to George VI's daughter and heir,
Elizabeth II, to make the first televised Christmas
message. It was a quarter of a century since her
grandfather George V began the tradition on radio. The
Queen was accommodated in the prime afternoon slot,
giving viewers a welcome glimpse of her home and its
décor, as well as her wardrobe and choice of jewellery.
Afterwards, *Billy Smart's Family Party* was scheduled,
featuring the chimps' tea party and the unrideable mule.

By now, Christmas television had made more inroads
into family festive celebrations, and the festive television
schedule became as much a part of the celebration as
mince pies and mulled wine. Comedy duo Morecambe
and Wise's *Christmas Show* of 1977 was dubbed the
most-watched television programme ever, attracting an
audience of twenty-eight million and featuring stars
including Elton John and the *Dad's Army* cast. Four years
later, the formula for compiling ratings changed, putting
a film at the top of the Christmas choices. In 1989,
Crocodile Dundee was watched by 21.77 million people.
However, the number two slot and six other places in
the top twenty belong to another British comedy show,
Only Fools and Horses, for shows made in the eighties
and nineties.

Out of Time but Not Out of Luck . . .

Bargain Hunt history was made when the crew went to Lancashire in 2021, where one of the strangest episodes ever made unfolded.

Caroline Hawley was guiding the blue team around a large emporium in Eccleston, with presenter Eric Knowles' challenge of buying at least one item 'with feet' in mind. Chartered surveyor Harry and Julia, a civil servant, were quick off the mark, buying a nineteenth-century brass sliding bevel for just £5. But after that they passed on various options until, with just eight minutes to go, they bought a second item. Both knew the boxed Lalique 'courting birds' was a relatively modern piece but still admired its distinctive charm and paid £119. The third purchase was a set of Royal Doulton plates featuring golfing figures, bought for £38, as the clock ran down.

But, if Caroline thought her team had got pulses racing by some last-minute dithering, opposite number Charles Hanson could top that tale.

He was shepherding the reds, administrator Geraldine and teacher Washington, around corridors and stairwells, drawing their attention to various items and hoping to find something 'with hands' to fulfil their challenge. But there seemed nothing upon which the couple could agree. It wasn't until almost half the time was up that they purchased the first item, a pair of wooden tennis racquets in presses, for just £9. As time dribbled away, Charles persuaded the couple to buy a Royal Doulton jug, dating from 1906 and made for the American market. There was a motto on its side, reading: 'May we never crack a joke to break a reputation.' Its rim anyway had certainly been comprehensively broken and, as a result, the price was just £5. Charles promised a profit on it.

But despite breaking out into a run, the team failed to make a third and final purchase, the first time that has ever happened in the twenty-one years that the show has been running. Not only that, the red team had failed to meet both their big spend challenge and their challenge to find an item with hands! Afterwards, Washington admitted: 'We were not very decisive.'

Still, Charles was not downhearted. 'I know we can come back from this,' he promised, as he pocketed £286, with which to purchase a bonus buy.

When it came to the auction, the blues made a flying start with a 'double bubble' result, as the bevel – bought for £5 – was sold for £10. But the frosted birds – which the couple thought was a pin tray but might have been an ashtray – was sold for just £35, presenting them with a substantial £84 loss. With the Royal Doulton golfing plates yielding a profit of just £2, they went with Caroline's bonus buy, a spindle-backed, ebonised child's chair, with gilt decorations and dating from Victorian times. She had paid £55 and presenter Eric was convinced it was a rare example. But it sold for just £10, leaving the blues with a figure of minus £122.

Yet, it looked likely to be sufficient for victory. As the red team had failed on the big spend, they had been penalised to the tune of £75 before their auction items even went under the gavel. And with just two items, even if either purchase made a profit, it was a huge mountain to climb to beat the blues!

Indeed, the two tennis racquets went for £10, making a profit of just £1. And even though the jug sold for £25, five times the purchase price, the couple were still at minus £54.

Their last roll of the dice lay with Charles' bonus buy, an Art Deco silver and enamel swivel desk clock. Washington took one look at it and presciently observed: 'It looks like it is in for the money. The escape is on.'

The clock cost a breathtaking £200 and the auctioneer Tom Blackmore thought it could be a risky move, valuing it at just £60–100. Geraldine and Washington watched, first in disbelief then outright joy, as the bidding raced ahead. And Charles and Eric joined them in elation when the hammer brought proceedings to an end, at £380. The reds ended up with a £126 profit and won the game.

Charles often promises contestants he will 'make a memory' with them on the show. This time, it was a roller-coaster that he would never forget.

'Never in my career has the emotion of *Bargain Hunt* set the heart racing so much,' he admitted.

17

CLOTHES, CLOTH AND LEATHER

Fast fashion – garments bought cheaply and worn once before being discarded – has a big impact on the environment.

The third-largest manufacturing industry in the world, the making of clothes is now thought to be responsible for up to 10 per cent of the world's carbon emissions, and 20 per cent of global waste water. Making clothes is believed to use more energy than aviation and shipping combined, while polyester takes hundreds of years to decompose. That's without giving due consideration to the conditions that some rag trade factory workers have to endure.

There's a significant push for fast fashion to be replaced by circular fashion, that's prolonging the life of clothing by selling it second hand. The share of the market inhabited by 'pre-loved' clothes is set to double from its 2020 figure of £18 billion to £39 billion in 2023.

Some clothes on sale are antiques, given their great age. The term 'vintage' is a grey area, with some people understanding that to mean anything made before the 1950s. For others, it means clothes made prior to the 1980s, while some use it interchangeably with the term 'second hand'.

Today, this kind of clothing is sold in shops, by charities, at flea markets, at car boot sales and online. With so many different outlets, the orthodox advice – to try before you buy – is difficult to follow as there may not be changing rooms at hand, with adequate lighting or three-way mirrors.

But when it comes to purchasing a pre-worn wardrobe, some of the *Bargain Hunt* experts need no persuasion.

Natasha Raskin Sharp champions vintage clothes to help conserve the planet's resources. For brides left blushing at the price of a new dress, she advises a visit to charity shops.

'Some people don't like the idea of a pre-worn wedding dress in case there is an emotional backstory to it. For me, there's a re-set at the point of sale. There's also an opportunity to re-work an existing dress, so when you walk up the aisle you will wearing something no one else has ever worn before.'

When it comes to buying vintage clothes, it's all about the armpits, says Natasha.

'Antiperspirant is a twentieth-century invention. So, prior to that – and even afterwards – it was the underarm area that took the most visible punishment. Sometimes white vinegar helps to remove stains like this. If not, you are going to have to make your peace with the marks or look into some alteration that masks it.'

But yesteryear's stains aren't the only consideration when it comes to buying clothes from an era when the hourglass figure was fashionable. Fitted garments from a bygone age tend to be considerably smaller, regardless of the sizing implied by the label.

'Beware when you buy vintage clothing online because the sizing system has changed. A skirt from the 1950s marked as a size 10 is considerably smaller than what we know to be a size 10 skirt in today's terms. Certainly, women had minute waists back then. But at the time they were also wearing corsetry and the boning made them smaller still. 'women's waists were narrower back then, but waist cinchers were still very popular at this time too.'

Wasp waist sizes mean there tend to be more 'tops' – blouses, jumpers and jackets – on sale, than 'bottoms' – trousers and skirts. Although later styles were more billowy, it remains essential to try garments on before buying whenever it's possible to do so.

Some outfits have survived for decades, simply because they are well constructed by comparison with today's clothes. Think piped seams, covered buttons, silk linings and bias-bound edges. Silk, linen, cotton and wool are firm favourites among buyers of classic clothes, but rayon – a synthetic fibre made from cellulose – also has a growing army of fans.

Mystery Object

What has two arms, three feet and doesn't move? The answer is a goffering iron, used to smooth ruffles, frills and flounces that the flat iron couldn't touch. Goffering irons like this one have hollow arms, into which a hot poker was inserted. Grasped in two hands, the crumpled material was then pulled firmly across the hot barrel to relieve it of creases. The implement was also called a tally iron, as it was introduced from Italy in the early seventeenth century. Goffering irons like this one, with two arms, are worth much more than single-limbed versions.

Also a fan of vintage clothes, Caroline Hawley fell in love with the red-and-gold paisley pattern on a suit dating from the seventies. The jacket fitted perfectly but the floor-length A-line skirt seemed unlikely to ever return to fashion. Undaunted, Caroline took it to a dressmaker who fashioned a pair of cigarette trousers out of the skirt. The outfit is now a firm favourite that she often wears on the show.

As far as vintage garments go, she advises, 'All antiques are sustainable and clothes are no different. The cut is better than modern clothes, the fabric is superior. Don't overlook second hand or charity shops when it comes to buying something special.'

Sizing can be an issue, she admits, but points out that unfitted styles are therefore a better option or, beyond that, look at hats and bags from bygone eras to make a style statement.

Her personal best buy was a Christian Dior fitted and boned silk dress, made in 1947, that she bought in a car boot sale for £4. The opportunity for that kind of deal happens rarely these days, with shops and stalls more aware than ever before about potential profit. And the pricing point can be problematic. Many people rail at paying high prices for clothes that have been worn before, forgetting that the seller has located it, researched its era and had it cleaned.

At both charity shops and auctions, it's worth looking out for big-name brands as second-hand garments will cost a fraction of new, although the cachet remains the same.

Sometimes shopping for vintage clothes feels like a treasure hunt – and there's a temptation to buy something that isn't a perfect fit. If there's a plan to employ a tailor to make the second-hand suit fit like a glove, that's fine. But don't splash your cash on something that will only come into use after significant alterations or losing half a stone.

Although Natasha advocates re-use rather than recycling, she sounds a note of caution about bringing moth infestations into the home. Carefully inspect clothing and ensure everything is suitably clean before it's put into the wardrobe.

Haunting vintage shops is likely to be more fruitful than buying in charity shops, where the great deals are likely hidden in an avalanche of clothing. Yet Natasha recalls, as a student, buying a pleated leather belt in a charity shop bearing the label of a major fashion retailer. Its cost off the peg at the time would have been about sixty times more than she paid, and she still uses it today.

Shopping for vintage clothes:

1. Check condition.

2. Use reputable dealers.

3. Double-check sizing.

4. Pick items that won't be damaged by average use.

5. Look for good labels.

6. Try it on before buying.

7. Store valuable clothes at home in acid-free paper, in boxes.

Sometimes older clothes on sale at auctions are not so much to wear but to collect. The contents of one wardrobe went under the hammer for £17,000 because the clothes had once belonged to Queen Victoria. Boots, bodices, a chemise, stockings, bloomers and a parasol were thought to have been given to photographer Alexander Lamont Henderson by servants after the monarch's death, in return for a personal photograph. His great, great grandson decided to declutter, and the clothing returned to a royal collection.

MENSWEAR

It's not just women's clothes available second hand, with men's suits made years ago tending to be much more durable than those produced today. Jackets are likely to be a better buy than shirts, though, for the propensity of thinner fabric to show wear and tear. Although sizing isn't always quite as crucial, it is important to remember that typically men today are taller and heavier than ever before.

Mystery Object

This gadget has two spindly arms, each with
different-shaped hooks at the ends, and belongs
to the era before zips. It's a button hook and boot
pull, used to do up the fiddly fasteners on spats,
gaiters, boots and stiff collars. Plain ones are
worth no more than £20, but those with ornate
handles, made in precious metals, and with
additional tools like scissors and shoe horns, will
fetch many times that sum.

With men's attire, you would end up with a very skewed
view if you judged what well-dressed chaps are wearing
today by a glance at *Bargain Hunt* buys. A London-made
top hat bought by one *Bargain Hunt* team for £30 sold
for exactly half price at auction. Yet a leather-lined
British National Fire Service helmet, dating from the
middle of the twentieth century, yielded a £15 profit,
after being bought for £40 and sold for £55.

OVERLOOKED AND UNDERVALUED

Napery – the blanket term for household linen,
particularly that used on tables – appears in 'job lots'
in removal boxes in weekly auctions across the country.
More often than not, very little detail about the boxes'

contents is listed in the catalogues. There's nothing better than heading down to the auction house in advance of the sale to inspect the box(es) for yourself. You might find that it's all worn and worthless, says Natasha, but it could well comprise reams of valuable Irish linen that's barely seen the light of day. 'It's unusual to come up against a lot of competition when you are bidding for textiles at auction,' she says. 'Although job lots like this can often contain truly quality material, they can sell for virtually nothing.'

BED COVERS

Today, most beds are covered with duvets. From the 1960s, the popularity of the so-called continental quilt gained traction, marginalising warm woollen blankets and tapestry quilts in the process. Finally, most of the makers went out of business. Still, Welsh wool blankets remain renowned for their quality, being built to last. A pink-and-green, double-sided blanket was bought by one team for £80, but the rosy glow that accompanied the purchase soon disappeared at auction, where it sold for a £20 loss. However, crafted blankets and quilts are now compared to an art form and those produced in Wales are elevated by special stitching patterns – rams' horns and church windows are often depicted; spirals almost always appear. Handmade items like this are a reflection of the quilter's individuality. As always, age and condition govern the price. However, a well-worn quilt can be given a second life as a cushion.

CASES AND TRUNKS

Leather bags, cases and trunks are popular buys among *Bargain Hunt* teams. A Gladstone bag – named for Prime Minister William Gladstone but best known as a doctor's case – was the subject-appropriate purchase for one of the celebrity editions, by *Casualty* actors Sunetra Sarker and Michael French. They patiently did a deal for just such a bag at £23, and sold it at auction for £140, yielding a £117 profit for charity. As Natasha observed, vintage leather – like fine wine – only gets better with age and leather goods like this can be brought back to life with relative ease, she revealed.

'Dry, old leather needs saddle soap and elbow grease. It will look completely different after a vigorous rub down.'

Some leather goods benefit from the 'lived-in' look. And while these days rucksacks are ergonomically designed to spread the load, it's not just doctors who will risk arm-ache for the style statement of a Gladstone bag, which, thanks to its hinged mouth, is sufficiently capacious even for travel.

There is a buoyant market for cases and trunks, but it's not among holidaymakers, as Natasha explains.

'You aren't seeing them on carousels at airports but rather in hotel lobbies and bedrooms, where they're up-cycled into bedside units or coffee tables. The larger the leather item, the more likely it is to be transformed into a piece of furniture, while smaller items are more likely to continue to fulfil their original purpose.'

Two vintage steamer trunks were bought by one *Bargain Hunt* team for £30 after expert Chuko Ojiri pointed out the possibilities for upcycling. Although the original paper lining of one was all but destroyed, with Chuko applying the description 'period condition', the second one was in better condition. Yet when it came to auction, none of the bidders saw the potential the buyers had invested their hopes in and, at £15, the pair of trunks went for half price.

SAMPLERS

Samplers – examples of embroidery that often feature a favourite homily – were another Regency novelty item frequently recreated after Queen Victoria came to the throne.

'Generally, the finer work was done pre-1837, in silks as opposed to wools,' says Caroline. 'But that means Victorian samplers are very reasonable in price; usually less than £50 will buy a piece of historic handiwork.'

With samplers, the strength of the colour in the thread can be key. Caroline has one that she found at a local village hall sale, tucked inside a pillowcase. Dated 1835 and in good condition, it ended with the lines, 'This is to let you see, what care my parents took of me.' The two final words were squeezed onto a different line. Caroline thinks it is probably worth between £300–500 today.

Bargain Hunt *in Numbers*

96 – the number of new episodes made each year

2,000 – the number of programmes made since *Bargain Hunt* began

392 – the number of people who go bargain hunting on the shows annually

30,000 – the number of teams that apply to take part each year

24 – the number of auction houses visited each year by the show

30 – the number of antiques fairs visited by the show

768 – the number of items selected for auction during the year

CONCLUSION

HOW DID THEY DO?

At the start of the book we left Katie and Aisha having completed their Bargain Hunt, tutored by Thomas who himself made a one pound bonus buy. The shopping hour had flashed passed but the contestants were committed to the purchases they had made, and harboured secret hopes of winning a golden gavel ....

First up was the bronze Buddha statue, which they had bought for £75. It went under the hammer for . . . £75. So, they didn't bank any profits, but nor did they record a damaging negative figure. Alas, after that their fortunes went south, with the 1940s' calculator bought for £35 and selling for just £20. And worse was to come, with the diamond-and-sapphire ring losing a mighty £94 at the auction. Thomas – who'd had just £1 to spend on his bonus buy – returned with a sherry bottle label. The good news was that it sold for £10, reducing this red team's loss to £109. It wasn't entirely plain sailing with Chuko's blue team either, which emerged from the auction with a shortfall of £61. However, with fewer losses, the blue team were that day's winners.

INDEX

Note: page numbers in **bold** refer to illustrations, page numbers in *italics* refer to information contained in tables.

Blackburn, Tony 251
Blackmore, Tom 301
blankets 313
Bliss, Kate 37–40, 55, 127, 150
board games 269–72
boats 86–7
bone china 22–3
books 203–5
boxes 161
Brearley, Harry 182
Bristol blue glass 107–8
British Army 241–2, 249
brooches 50, 52
buckles 124–5
Buddha statues 3
Bugatti 225
butter shapers 180
button cleaners 249–50
button hook and boot pull 312

cake-breakers 231, **231**
calculators 4
calling cards 142–3
cameo glass 108
cameras 3–4
Cameron, John 31, 53–4, 77,
    92, 117, 133, 170, 185,
    200, 214, 238, 245, 248–9,
    256
cannon balls 251
cars 89, 225
    toy 70–2, 73
cases 314–15
catchphrases 8
ceramics 9–33, 199, 217
chairs 158, 166–9, 224, 232
    children's 159
    fold-down 87
character jugs 28–30, 273–4
cheroots 139–40

chess 269–71
chests 161
Chinese wares 12–17, 83–4,
    87–8, 217
Chinoiserie 4, 14
Chippendale, Thomas 157–8
Christian Dior 309
Christmas memorabilia 283–97
cigarette cards 266–8
cleaning agents 177
Cliff, Clarice 23–5, **24**
clocks 275–82, 301
clothes/cloth 303–16
club swinging 268
Codd bottles 115
coinage 81, 250–1
Cole, Sir Henry 287–8
collectors 233–4
components 92
condition 22–3, 55, 200, 217,
    234
Connell, Stephanie 11, 88, 164,
    180, 192–3, 231–4, 281
construction techniques 92,
    133–4
Cooper, Ben 14–15, 47–8,
    106–7, 130–1
Cooper, Susie 25
copper pans 175–8
craftmanship 117–18
cricket memorabilia 265–6, 267
cruet sets 178–9
cutlery
    silver collars 132
    see also spoons

dating antiques 121
Davis, Harry 19, 20
death pennies 244
Delftware 13

Hogben, Michael 21
Hornby 68–9, 70
horse groomers 147, **147**

IKEA 164
Irvine, Roo 23–5, 28–9, 44–6,
    65, 67, 98–100, 103,
    111–2, 131, 169, 216, 228,
    252–3, 269, 288–9

Jacobean glass 103
Jacobsen, Arne 167
Japonism 17
jet 44–5
jewellery 4–5, 35–52
    cleaning 50
Johnson, George 21

kintsugi 17
kitchens 173–82
Knowles, Eric 23, 25–6, 101,
    107–9, 113, 150, 298,
    300–1
Kodak, Box Brownie 4

Laidlaw, Paul viii
Lalique 110–12, 298
Lanterloo (game) 160
laundry accessories 180–1
lead crystal 99
leather 303–16
Leonard Collection 27
life expectancy 232–3

Mackintosh, Charles Rennie
    227, 228
Madley, Richard 74–5, 178,
    196, 265–6, 271
mangles 180–1
marbles 267–8

Märklin 68
"Mary Gregory" art glass 108
matches 140–2
materials 53–6, 133–4
Matthews, Tom 241–2
Mauchline 90
Measham 27
measurements 214
Meccano 68–9
mechanical pencils 145–6
medals 245–9
medium 53–6
menswear 311–12
mid-twentieth-century furniture
    164, 165–7
Mikimoto, Kokichi 41
militaria 239–55
Mills, Nathaniel 142, 143
Minton Hollins 26
modern art 197
monarchs, British 31, *32–3*
Moorcroft 26
Morris, William 177, 223–4
mourning jewellery 44–5
Mouseman 163
Murano glass 98–9
musical instruments 206–10

napery 312–13
Newport Potteries 23
Nuwar, Steve 246, 247

oak 156, 162–3
object identification 77–8
Ojiri, Chuko 5, 72, 131, 142,
    315
Omega 281–2

paintings 194–9
pans, copper 175–8